Also by David L. Bahnsen

The Case for Dividend Growth:
Investing in a Post-Crisis World

Crisis of Responsibility:
Our Cultural Addiction to Blame and How You Can Cure It

There's No Free Lunch

250 ECONOMIC TRUTHS

There's No Free Lunch

—250—
ECONOMIC
TRUTHS

DAVID L. BAHNSEN

PostHill
PRESS

A POST HILL PRESS BOOK

There's No Free Lunch:

250 Economic Truths

© 2021 by David L. Bahnsen

All Rights Reserved

ISBN: 978-1-63758-014-1

ISBN (eBook): 978-1-63758-015-8

Cover art by Mina Widmer

Illustrations by Sarah Jane Souther

Post Hill Press
New York • Nashville
posthillpress.com

Published in the United States of America

2 3 4 5 6 7 8 9 10

DEDICATION

This book is dedicated to Eric Balmer and Aaron Bradford.

Far more than my "Triple B book club" companions for over fifteen years, you have been my brothers and friends for nearly thirty years. I am a better person as a result of having you both in my life. There are no words to capture the gratitude I have for you and your love for me.

May you flourish daily in freedom and virtue, cherishing the good life we all care about so dearly.

TABLE OF CONTENTS

INTRODUCTION

One of the challenges in understanding economics, or for that matter, teaching it, is first defining it. There are all sorts of subjects and disciplines where intelligent men and women disagree over particulars, but few I can think of where the basic definition of the subject is disagreeable. I am convinced that a substantial amount of the travesty of economic teaching permeating today starts with a flawed definition that is attempting to be taught.

Dylan Pahman defines an economy as "the cultivation of creation, through human labor, for the provision of human needs, through relationships of exchange." This captures the essence of the great contribution from Ludwig Von Mises—that fundamentally economics is the study of "human action." Pahman adds the anthropological necessity to how we understand human action as the basis for economics, and he specifies the area of human action that is distinctly economic—that is, relationships of exchange.

It is my desire in this book to present basic truths of economics, and yet if economics were what we are told it is today—a series of metrics and formulas intended to optimize the distribution of scarce resources—the book would primarily be a math or science book. This book is not a math or science book, because economics is not a math or science discipline.

Vladimir Lenin famously said that any business could be run by "anybody who can read and write and knows the first four rules of arithmetic." His egalitarian worldview that desired everyone "doing the same work and receiving the same wages" only partially explains his tragically flawed view of what a business was and how it could succeed. Lenin's fundamental flaw was not understanding the *humanity* of a business, which is to say, the *innovation and creativity* that drive enterprise.

But even that can be restated more accurately this way: Lenin (and all socialist/Marxist/collectivists) failed to understand that man is created in the image of God. Business cannot be reduced to the commoditized functions of technocratic operations, because business flows from the creative spirit of mankind, and the creative spirit of mankind comes from our status as image-bearers of God. If you get this wrong, you will get everything else wrong. Lenin is case in point.

So it is with the broad study of economics. Not only do our business endeavors in the modern context of professional pursuits stem from important truths about the human person, but so does everything that forms civilization. It has always been so. My vision for this book is not merely to address contemporary controversies in the context of human action but the entire foundation of the field—its aim, its purpose, its end.

As you will see in the very first section of truths presented, human flourishing is the aim of my study of economics. I do not believe a secular view of markets, divorced from the dignity of mankind which flows out of creation, can lead to the kind of human flourishing for which our hearts yearn. A secular view of markets can be thought of as right-wing (Randian) or left-wing (collectivist), but both stand together in failing to put the focus on the dignity of the human person—a dignity understood best by viewing man as image bearers of God. God is *the* creator and innovator, and man, as His image-bearer, is to be creative and innovative. If we never studied another thing about economics but understood that, we could do far, far worse.

I chose the topics that I did to organize these economic truths because I believe they synthesize opportunity for application with key first principles. I do not want a student of economics to consider minimum wage laws without first understanding basic principles of economics, and yet there is no point in studying the principles of economics without the ability to apply them to issues such as minimum wage laws.

I would suggest that the vast majority of poor economic policies we have seen over the years do not come from those who disbelieved key principles, but rather those who failed to consistently apply the principles they claim to believe in to matters of application. These subjects can be messy, complicated, and lead to temptations to sway from our belief system. What I want this book to do is help solidify one's belief system about economics and aid in that application to the messy issues of our day.

I have tried my best to limit use of obscure or esoteric vocabulary in the book. Some expressions may seem awkward at first glance ("the knowledge problem"), but I hope they will be defined and explained in such a way that you will see the indispensability of the framework. Using that very example, it is the "knowledge problem" (how information is best seen and understood in a society) that is the basis for my view of a market economy, of a limited role of the state in such, and for basic doctrines of social organization. The verbiage is all intended to be adequate for the task of explanation and formation without becoming excessive in complexity.

This book contains quotes from a plethora of people, and I don't mind saying that the vast majority of them are masters. These are largely "cream of the crop" economists who have substantially informed my economic worldview, but who also have substantially informed economic policy, debate, and discussion in some cases for centuries. That said, there should be no assumption that I agree with every individual and every other thing they advocated. And there should be no assumption that each individual

I quote would agree with one another on every issue. I largely avoided those whose overall net contribution to public thought I mostly disagree with (there may be one or two exceptions). But even where I agree with 60–95 percent of someone's intellectual contributions, that leaves some areas where I may disagree. The only assurance I can offer you is that where I quote a given author, I surely agree with what I have quoted. The book's subtitle is "250 Economic Truths" for a reason—I believe this book is made up of truthful statements about economics, and I have tried to provide truthful commentary around each statement.

In the year this book has been written, we are somehow engaged in a great debate over basic matters of freedom and agency in our market economy. Individual responsibility's stock is trading at a lower and lower level. Class warfare is at a high, and many on the right are joining those on the left in disdain for economic achievement. A materialistic view of poverty alleviation rules throughout the culture, one that neither alleviates poverty, nor solves for the woes of what truly ails mankind.

I am unwilling to view the subject of taxation or the size of government as merely "econometric." Measurements of Gross Domestic Product (GDP) may serve a data purpose in some analysis, but they are not the aim of economic study. We care about economic growth because we care for the human person, and the human person can flourish when they are free to grow and prosper. What optimizes this aim is my desire, and what impedes this aim is my enemy. If and where increased government spending impedes future economic growth, it needs to be understood and analyzed for that purpose—not as a mere data analysis.

There are two leading trends in economics right now that must be resisted. One is the mystifying movement towards greater collectivism as a means of improving the needs of the underprivileged. It is a futile and dangerous effort, but one that can do great damage as it is embraced. The other is a sort of apathy or complacency about sound economics from those who know better. This apathy would be forgivable if economics were merely math, merely formulaic, merely academic. But it is the well-being of humanity on the line, and our recent amnesia of what the stakes are in this debate runs the risk of doing great harm to civilization.

> *"The times call for courage. The times call for hard work. But if the demands are high, it is because the stakes are even higher. They are nothing less than the future of human liberty, which means the future of civilization."*
>
> *- Henry Hazlitt*

It is far too easy to lose passion for that which has enabled our abundance and prosperity when we are so engulfed in the blessings of our abundance and prosperity. Our tasting of the tree of a market economy does not actually require us to know how the tree was planted.

> *"We do not need to understand economics in order to experience the benefits of freedom of exchange and production. But we may very well need to understand economics in order to sustain and maintain the institutional framework that enables us to realize the benefits that flow from freedom of exchange and production."*
>
> *- Peter J. Boettke*

The debate over economics today is not one that just threatens the fruit from the tree, but the tree itself. The ongoing maintenance of the framework that has allowed for such unprecedented prosperity requires a review of first principles and a reaffirmation of the applications that come from these principles. Engaging this cause intellectually is a great adventure, as Hayek said, but it also is a moral imperative.

I hope this book will establish, review, remind, and encourage. It is not exhaustive, nor could it be if I had wanted such. Each subject invites more granularity, more detailed study, and more debate. Yet I am convinced that such study and debate will greatly benefit from these 250 economic truths.

So will the cause of human flourishing.

HUMAN FLOURISHING

"I wish to preach, not the doctrine of ignoble ease, but the doctrine of the strenuous life, the life of toil and effort, of labor and strife; to preach that highest form of success which comes, not to the man who desires mere easy peace, but to the man who does not shrink from danger, from hardship, or from bitter toil, and who out of these wins the splendid ultimate triumph."

- Theodore Roosevelt

If I could only leave readers of this book with one message on the glory of free enterprise, it would not be about monetary policy, tax rates, supply and demand, or marginal utility. All of those things matter, and all of them, plus so much more, will be addressed throughout this book. But the *main thing* is this—the human flourishing that feeds the soul of mankind through earned success. In this sense, I write not merely about the system of market-based economics, or even its societal value. I write about the existential value to human beings that comes from freedom, from adversity, and from the freedom to conquer adversity.

"Our faith in freedom does not rest on the foreseeable results in particular circumstances but on the belief that it will, on balance, release more forces for the good than for the bad."

- F.A Hayek

Human flourishing is the goal in a free and virtuous society, but utopian perfection is not. In this distinction may exist the key issue separating the most ghastly of failed economic visions from the one that has unleashed the most prosperous results in world history. An acceptance of imperfectibility is vital if we are to flourish. We cannot cut off the forces of good that can permeate far and wide for the long term because we do not like the result in an isolated and narrow situation in the short term.

"Human liberty—and not the machinery of coercion or investment, or even by science itself—is what made for a great enrichment, from 1800 to the present... Liberated people devising new technologies and institutions did an amazing job from 1800 to the present and will keep doing it. Liberty will make the enrichment worldwide. And the Enrichment will not corrupt the human soul."

- Deirdre McCloskey

That the world spent many thousands of years in what would be considered "poverty conditions" (on a basic absolute basis) is indisputable. And that a consistent and profound increase in the absolute level of riches has been the story of the last two hundred years is also indisputable. The correlation here is causation—the advent of liberty, first in Western Europe and then to the shores of the colonies. In those pockets of world geography, where liberalism had been unleashed, profound enrichment followed.

"Under capitalism the common man enjoys amenities which in ages gone by were unknown and therefore inaccessible even to the richest people. But, of course, these motorcars, television sets and refrigerators do not make a man happy. In the instant in which he acquires them, he may feel happier than he did before. But as soon as some of his wishes are satisfied, new wishes spring up. Such is human nature."

- Ludwig Von Mises

The reality of human nature to which Von Mises speaks here is a primary reason to avoid materialistic foundations to defend free enterprise. The consumption of a good brings us temporal happiness; the production of a good can bring us dignifying satisfaction (as image bearers of the ultimate creator). The aim of free enterprise (and the aim of her defenders) must never be the mere temporal happiness that comes from a satisfying bite of food or intrigue that comes from use of a new technology. Rather, it is the human flourishing that freedom and our productive capacity are most qualified to bring. And human flourishing is exponentially deeper and wider than a mere sugar-high from a consumer product.

"To the extent that the years between the end of World War II and today are a story of competing economic visions, the short version is this: Karl Marx was wrong, and Milton Friedman was right. Market-oriented reforms over the past several decades have cut severe poverty around the world by more than half. As late as 1980, more than 40% of the world's population lived in severe poverty, according to World Bank figures. Now, that share is less than 10%. There is simply nothing else in the history of the material affairs of the world that can compare to that."

- Kevin Williamson

Marx vs. Friedman (or Marx vs. Smith) is a useful framing of the subject of this book, though perhaps more simplistic than I prefer. And as a prima facie glance into the fruits on the tree of each respective school of thought, one can do worse than to look at what free enterprise has meant in reducing poverty versus the collective well-being conditions of the Communist Bloc countries. If the most rapid reduction in extreme poverty in world history is not prima facie reason to embrace market economics, I stand confused as to what our aim here is.

"No society can surely be flourishing and happy, of which the far greater part of the members are poor and miserable."

- Adam Smith

This is true both morally and economically. Man as moral agents must pursue conditions of flourishing for all. And while the utopian vision is futile on this side of glory, in a society of free exchange, incentives exist that result in conditions of flourishing and commercial satisfaction for the vast majority of the citizenry. Poverty may not be fully eradicated, but it will not be the majority condition of the society.

"We must make the building of a free society once more an intellectual adventure, a deed of courage.... Unless we can make the philosophic foundations of a free society once more a living intellectual issue, and its implementation a task which challenges the ingenuity and imagination of our liveliest minds, the prospects of freedom are indeed dark. But if we can regain that belief in the power of ideas which was the mark of liberalism at its best, the battle is not lost."

- F.A. Hayek

I can honestly say that when I first read this from Hayek decades ago, my life changed. "An intellectual adventure," indeed. No quest can bring about more flourishing of the human spirit than to succeed in a deed of courage, and those who would engage the intellectual battle against all odds for the liberal society will certainly require courage. But ideas rooted in truth make possible human flourishing. And the tenets of freedom, voluntary exchange, individual responsibility, and the dignity of mankind created in the image of God are all rooted in truth. Ours is an intellectual and moral adventure, indeed.

"Successful companies create value by providing products or services their customers value more highly than available alternatives. They do this while consuming fewer resources, leaving more resources available to satisfy other needs in society. Value creation involves making people's lives better. It is contributing to prosperity in society."

- Charles G. Koch

Our defense of free enterprise must always come from this sequence and explanation of objectives. The aim of value creation is serving others, because without the service of others, there is no value creation. The alignment of interests between both sides of an economic exchange and the prosperity that creates at scale is the basis for our free enterprise defense.

"Opulent, civilized, and industrious nations, are greater consumers than poor ones, because they are infinitely greater producers."

- Jean-Baptiste Say

The cause and effect here is so important. While we can't help but envy consumption, and note the satisfaction that consumption of wants brings, we must note that great consumers are always and forever, first, great producers. The opulence, civility, and industry they enjoy comes only anecdotally from consumption, but at a far deeper level, from their capacity for production, which economically makes consumption possible and existentially brings purpose.

"Man naturally desires, not only to be loved, but to be lovely; or to be that thing which is the natural and proper object of love. He naturally dreads, not only to be hated, but to be hateful; or to be that thing which is the natural and proper object of hatred. He desires, not only praise, but praiseworthiness; or to be that thing which, though it should be praised by nobody, is, however, the natural and proper object of praise. He dreads, not only blame, but blameworthiness; or to be that thing which, though it should be blamed by nobody, is, however, the natural and proper object of blame."

- Adam Smith

What is at stake in centralized control economics is nothing less than the loveliness of man. The desires of our fallen nature are tamed to some degree (not entirely) by market forces, and our longings for love, loveliness, and reputation are enhanced and served by market forces. Our moral sentiments do not merely care for our public reputation but must be cultivated to care for what we know to be true of ourselves. A market economy most cultivates human flourishing when these sentiments are most elevated.

"[The market] makes human relations more dignified. The system of exchange, as opposed to the more aristocratic system of owner and tenant, allows even the less privileged to address society in terms of what they have to offer, rather than what they need ... abject dependence upon the benevolence of others is demoralizing. Extending the rule of the market to all helps most men avoid this fate and so allows them to function as dignified equals."

- Yuval Levin

The way in which human dignity is respected by this process is hard to overstate. Market exchange equalizes the two parties in that they both have something to offer, and both have a need or want to be satisfied. The welfare state, a redistributionist accord, and the pre-enlightenment feudal system all share an inferiority to the market system in that they reframe the role of one economic actor to that of a subordinate. A market economy allows for dignity and civility.

"When you're in a situation where people are bringing you things constantly, your entrepreneurial skills are dulled and your whole culture becomes deadened. Your personhood is disrespected."

- Father Robert Sirico

Human flourishing is simply impossible for someone who is made to be a beggar, a pure recipient of the productive activities of others. Economic policy that seeks to turn a person into an object essentially strips away human dignity and reflects disdain for the human person. A high regard for the human person wants to see material needs met but never at the expense of existential, spiritual, and emotional ones. A free and virtuous society solves for the physical, but even more so—for the anthropological.

"In every age everybody knows that up to his own time, progressive improvement has been taking place; nobody seems to reckon on any improvement in the next generation. We cannot absolutely prove that those are in error who say society has reached a turning point—that we have seen our best days. But so said all who came before us and with just as much apparent reason.... On what principle is it that with nothing but improvement behind us, we are to expect nothing but deterioration before us?"

- Thomas Babington Macaulay

Those who bemoan the future conditions of despair that free enterprise are "sure" to produce—environmentally, socially, morally—boldly do so against the testimony of history and common sense.

"A culture of the casual is a culture of people who already have achieved something and who already can prove it. It is a culture of the static and the settled, the opposite of Tocqueville's restless Americans."

-Tyler Cowen

Human flourishing never has as its aim the "casualness" of modern, consumer life. It strives for something better, and what is better in the "good life" is the restless productivity of being adventurous, of being creative, of being ambitious, of being more.

"By contrast, keep on with various versions of old-fashioned monarchy, or with slow or fast socialism, with its betterment-killing policies protecting the favored classes, especially the rich or the Party or the cousins, Bad King John or Robin Hood—in its worst forms a military socialism or a tribal tyranny, and even in its best a stifling regulation of new cancer drugs—and you get the grinding routine of human tyranny and poverty, with their attendant crushing of the human spirit. The agenda of modern liberalism, ranged against tyranny and poverty, is achieving human flourishing in the way it has always been achieved. Let my people go. Let ordinary people have a go. Stop pushing people around."

- Deirdre N. McCloskey

An economic order not rooted in liberty is bound to fail whether its stated aim is punishing the rich or rewarding the rich and powerful, because any economic order not rooted in liberty crushes the human spirit. It is when humans are free to act that society has seen vertical mobility. In all contrary systems, we are only debating about the severity of the soul-crushing results.

"Economic control is not merely control of a sector of human life which can be separated from the rest; it is the control of the means for all our ends. And whoever has sole control of the means must also determine which ends are to be served, which values are to be rated higher and which lower, in short, what men should believe and strive for."

- F.A. Hayek

I can think of no greater impediment to the cause of human flourishing than to grant to the state authority over how we accomplish what we set to accomplish as a society. Some would say that worse than giving the state the power over the means is the power to select the ends themselves—to set the actual agenda. But the fact of the matter is that once you grant the state control over the means, you have given them control over the ends, inevitably and inseparably. This has crushed the cause of human flourishing, as the purpose of mankind had been distorted in what has been an entirely foreseeable chain of events.

"Most of America's leading entrepreneurs are bound to the masts of their fortunes. They are allowed to keep their wealth only as long as they invest it in others. In a real sense, they can keep only what they give away. It has been given to others in the form of investments. It is embodied in a vast web of enterprises that retains its worth only through constant work and sacrifice. Capitalism is a system that begins not with taking but with giving to others."

- George Gilder

This so beautifully encapsulates the connection between free enterprise and human flourishing. The very incentives of a market economy first promote flourishing by demanding service to others if one is to meet profitability in the marketplace. But then, having achieved wealth, capital is deployed in the very markets that drive future growth and prosperity. Successful entrepreneurs may choose to bury their money or burn their money, providing little social benefit after the first act; but that would be perilous to their own self-interest! The system itself would never intend such. Rather, it incents reinvestment, the pursuit of further return on investment, and thus activities that inevitably better those around him or her, as well.

"It is good luck to be born in America ... The 'luck' consists chiefly of a modern liberal ideology of innovism combined with reasonably honest courts and reasonably secure property rights and reasonably non-extractive governments and reasonably effective educational systems, and a reasonably long time for the reasonably good ideas, and especially the innovations, to do their work. By all means let's spread the good luck around— by persuading people to a modern liberalism leading to the Great Enrichment, and a full life."

- Deirdre N. McCloskey

Rather than bemoan those who had the good fortune to be born in a country that has made the necessary decisions to cultivate human flourishing, let us seek to spread that formula around. We ought to study and understand what has created such wealth in America, seek more of the same domestically, and share the secret sauce with the world at large. We are embracing in the modern context a shame or embarrassment for our good fortunes. Care for mankind would demand that we do the opposite—present with pride a belief in innovation, freedom, and the good life.

"We have always been concerned that economic education—a real understanding of how a market functions—will first and foremost help the most vulnerable.... Obviously, what helps the poor is access to work. But as we looked into the good intentions of so many people, we see that a lot of them just think that solidarity with poor people means giving them things, and from our understanding of how markets function, and from our understanding of human beings, you really find that human beings themselves are the producers of their own wealth and of their own way out of poverty. [We must show] how wealth is created, and that the nature of people even in the middle of their poverty is to be creative and produce more than they consume. That's what's called wealth: When you produce more than you consume."

- Father Robert Sirico

An entire book could (and should) come from the sentiment of what Father Sirico expresses here. The poverty cure comes from production, which means the cultivation of the human spirit manifested in skills and productive capacity. When one has the ability to produce, they have the capacity to generate wealth. Centering an economic worldview around consumption is man-focused in the most trite and simplistic of ways; but developing an entire ecosystem of thought and action around production, well that honors the human person, and opens the door to a sustainable, soul-giving eradication of poverty.

"The question is not whether we wish to see everybody as well off as possible. Among men of good will such an aim can be taken for granted. The real question concerns the proper means of achieving it. And in trying to answer this we must never lose sight of a few elementary truisms. We cannot distribute more wealth than is created. We cannot in the long run pay labor as a whole more than it produces."

- Henry Hazlitt

This is human flourishing brought to the title of this book. My aim in promoting a free and virtuous society is the cause of human flourishing. And yet, I do not advance that aim—only falsehood—by pretending that there is a free lunch out there. Once we accept the reality of trade-offs in our understanding of economics, we will not inhibit the cause of human flourishing, we will instead make it actually feasible.

"We need to begin to make a way forward about the fundamental things most human beings are agreed about when it comes to the human person. If you interviewed a hundred people and asked them one question: 'do you believe that human life has intrinsic dignity?' I bet you would get nearly universal agreement to that question. And if you could expand on that question to other shared visions about what a human being is for, what the purpose of work is, what opportunities should look like, and why people should have those opportunities, then together we might be able to stop thinking about this construction—economic man—and instead think about our purpose, and what we're for, beyond avoiding work, beyond consumption, beyond doing things that only last for today."

- Victor Claar

I can think of no better way to conclude this section. Human flourishing is not about a man of transactions, the mere allocation of scarce resources. When we accept the dignity of mankind as the foundation of our adventure, we begin to ask the right questions and pursue deeper answers that satisfy the longings of our soul.

HUMAN ACTION

"Human civilization is not something achieved against nature; it is rather the outcome of the working of the innate qualities of man."

- Ludwig Von Mises

I can summarize what economics is this way: Man was made in the image of God, with properties of independence, creativity, aspiration, and self-preservation. The actions of man as created beings reflect man's internal qualities, and in the aggregate form, civilizations. Human action is economics, and economics is human action. At the root of economics will always be the human person, not a mathematical model. Indeed, at the root of civilization will always be the failures and triumphs of mankind.

"To understand our civilization, one must appreciate that the extended order resulted not from human design or intention but spontaneously: it arose from unintentionally conforming to certain traditional and largely moral practices, many of which men tend to dislike, whose significance they usually fail to understand, whose validity they cannot prove, and which have nonetheless fairly rapidly spread by means of an evolutionary selection—the comparative increase of population and wealth—of those groups that happened to follow them."

- F.A. Hayek

This is human action at its finest and its fullest—man acting in freedom and individuality, but out of the miracle of God's created order, seeing civilization formed. Understanding but then appreciating the dynamic of human action as both spontaneous in its individual expressions but the source of order in its collective result is critical in understanding economics.

"The Enrichment wasn't achieved by government coercion, which is usually counterproductive.... Nor was it achieved by science unassisted, or the exploitation of slaves, or the routine accumulation of capital, or a profound dialectic of history.... It was achieved by liberty alone, a necessary and pretty much sufficient cause.... Give people liberty, and by uncoerced cooperation through commerce they become adults, enriched in body and soul."

- Deirdre McCloskey

What McCloskey has said here provides us valuable reinforcement—liberty facilitated greater human action, and out of greater human action came enrichment. A freer mankind, acting with capacity, agency, and incentive, raised the standard of living exponentially upon absorption of this greater freedom. But McCloskey says that liberty was "pretty much" sufficient— an inadequate but telling qualifier. Yes, liberty enabled free exchange, and in such cooperative effort, adulthood is needed. But it is that coupling of freedom to virtue, to responsibility, to cooperation, to integrity, to morality, to trust, that became the potent formula. Liberty incentivizes it. Liberty is a necessary condition for it. But liberty alone is not sufficient. Liberty coupled with virtue becomes the ideal recipe for prosperity.

"I would criticize Keynes as having an empty anthropology altogether. Flawed anthropologies lead to flawed economic policy, and you can see this flawed anthropology today in the Fed's dual mandate... [of] full employment and price stability. This isn't economics as deep moral theory anymore; this is economics as a video game. How can we tinker with the federal funds rate in order to manipulate the scoreboard with all the macro economic variables on it to get the outcomes that we like, and that make us look good...when we forget about the individuals who are trying to make plans. And sometimes those top-down policy actions frustrate the individual decision making that happens at the more personal level."

- Victor Claar

You will notice that he takes on a lot of topics here—the anthropology of Keynesianism, the lack of wisdom in the dual mandate of the Fed, attempts to top-down control the economy, etc. But ultimately, everything comes down to one thing here—the impediments to human action that stem from top-down interventionism. And I do not merely mean impediments to efficiency—logistical impediments (and neither does Claar). Above all else, policy actions that frustrate human action take grave risk in impeding the cause of human flourishing.

"The process of discovery begins when we observe, often vaguely, a gap between what is and what could be. Our intuition tells us something better is just beyond the range of our mind's eye. To build a culture of discovery, we must encourage, not discourage, the passionate pursuit of hunches (no matter their origin)."

- Charles G. Koch

This inquisitive component of human nature is God-created, and out of this process comes miraculous things. Human observation transcends that of the animals, who may very well observe basic empirical realities but lack the soulful capacity for bridging the gap between what is and what could be. Humans were given not just this ability but this burden—this opportunity—this cultural mandate.

"The more information that's out there, the greater the returns to just being willing to sit down and apply yourself. Information isn't what's scarce; it's the willingness to do something with it."

- Tyler Cowen

This is the heart of economics as human action—no information or gathering of information is worth a hill of beans apart from the human action brought to the information. Tenacity, creativity, and initiative create wealth; information is as abundant as sand.

"The ultimate ends of the activities of reasonable beings are never economic. Money is one of the greatest instruments of freedom ever invented by man."

- F.A. Hayek

Humans act. They act out of pursuit of their dreams, their quests, their aspirations. Money provides an instrument in that action, but it is not, and can never be, the essence of the action itself. We develop a more exhaustive understanding of economics when we study the actions that undergird human endeavor and resist the temptation to reduce the field to mathematical and monetary measurements.

"All rational action is, in the first place, individual action. Only the individual thinks. Only the individual reasons. Only the individual acts."

- Ludwig Von Mises

You are seeing here a key philosophical tenet in market economics vs. Marxian collectivism. A high view of human dignity leads to a high view of the individual—of man as unique and special in his or her context as an image-bearer of God. The Marxian view is that history is inevitable and unconcerned with the individual. Material forces will bring the individual along, but the individual will play no noteworthy role in the direction of mankind. The subordination of the individual to a collective is a foundational view of those who oppose free enterprise. That collectives reflect the rational acts of individuals is the foundational view of those who cherish free enterprise.

"Economics teaches you that making a choice means giving up something. And economics can help you appreciate complexity and how seemingly unrelated actions and people can become entangled."

- Russ Roberts

That making a choice means giving up something is not just the "there's no free lunch" part of economics in one phrase. It is the essence of human action being the foundation of economics. Humans act, and in so acting, they make choices, every second of the day. The choices they make that flow out of the basic functions of human action reflect a constant weighing of costs vs. benefits. Some of these decisions happen in nano-seconds with no apparent consciousness behind them. Some are more deliberative and process-driven. But at its core, economics is both the living out of giving up something to receive something (in minor, inconsequential categories, or more significant ones), and the invisible entanglements of human actions with other human actions. This social cooperation starts with a human acting and becomes a whole lot of humans acting—individually, and with collective consequence. This, my friends, is economics.

"Capitalism does not merely mean that the housewife may influence production by her choice between peas and beans; or that plant managers have some voice in deciding what and how to produce: it means a scheme of values, an attitude toward life, a civilization—the civilization of inequality and of the family fortune."

- Joseph A. Schumpeter

Free enterprise is a holistic concept, the sum total of human action, the process of allocating scarce resources, the attitudes and values that shape such actions, and the civilization which can come out of freedom and virtue.

"The free market is not a system. It is not a policy dictated by anyone in particular. It is not something that Washington implements. It does not exist in any legislation, law, bill, regulation, or book. It is what you get when people act on their own, entirely without central direction, and with their own property, and within human associations of their own creation and in their own interest. It is the beauty that emerges in absence of control."

- Jeffrey Tucker

Free enterprise, then, is the natural outflow of *human action*. Before there are interventions, regulations, stipulations, controls, or red tape—there are humans acting, associating, cooperating, building, and creating. The belief in man as a co-creator with God, the result of being made in His own image, drives me to believe that the human action a free enterprise system cultivates best honors his or her personhood and dignity. Out of the creative and free capacity of a humanity not living in servitude, has mankind done her best work.

"In a commercial world, we bump regularly against strangers, but the strangers become friends. To my friends the communitarians I say: your sweet ends are achieved precisely by commerce."
- Deirdre N. McCloskey

Rather than demonize business, we ought to embrace the social reality that community is enhanced by trade and commerce. To believe that we create fuller communities by denying them free exchange with one another is to assert the idiotic. In the context of commercial endeavors, true friendships can be born—not always, but certainly often. In the context of a commerce-free world, social alienation is assured.

"Today most of the debate on the cutting edge in macro-economics would not call itself 'Keynesian' or 'mone-tarist' or any other label relating to a school of thought. The data are considered the ruling principle, and it is considered suspect to have too strong a loyalty to any particular model about the underlying structure of the economy."

- Tyler Cowen

Cowen may be saying this prescriptively, as if it were a good thing. Or he may be saying it descriptively, merely observing what has become the case in modern economic debate. But what it is must surely be called an abject disaster, where the arrogance of "data dependency" pretends to work from no ideological framework—no belief system—no intellectual commitments or assertions. Post-enlightenment economics have seen numerous errors in thought, but those errors have largely had a label attached to them, making identification and avoidance all the easier. There is no more dangerous error in economics than one hiding behind the disingenuity of anonymous love of data. Econometricism is just as philosophical as any other -ism and worse than others in its lack of self-awareness. The effort to replace the human action of economics with a spreadsheet is the most ignorant and arrogant development in the history of economic error.

"We can never at one and the same time question all [traditional] values. Such absolute doubt could lead only to the destruction of our civilization and—in view of the numbers to which economic progress has allowed the human race to grow—to extreme misery and starvation. Complete abandonment of all traditional values is, of course, impossible; it would make man incapable of acting."

- F.A. Hayek

Human action flows out of value systems. Those who hold traditional values in disdain have every right to put the burden of legitimacy on those who hold to them. But human action throughout history has led to greater growth and less misery. Those who would dismiss the traditions and values that have accompanied human action throughout civilization carry a burden themselves—accounting for what value system will replace that which we dismiss without wreaking havoc on civilization. It's a tall order.

"Capitalists are motivated not chiefly by the desire to consume wealth or indulge their appetites, but by the freedom and power to consummate their entrepreneurial ideas."

- George Gilder

Anyone who has spent any time with the serial entrepreneur knows this to be true—that while the profit motive and quality of life considerations drive ambition to a degree, they can't hold a candle to the innate desire to act, produce, create, and grow. The delivery and execution of an idea is at the heart of successful entrepreneurship, and profits merely follow. Somewhere in all of this will be consumption, yet fundamentally the driver of entrepreneurship is always the combination of the vision, dream, and passion of the entrepreneur.

*"By contrast, human action, to use the 'Austrian' eco-
nomic term, is not merely reactive to constraints and
utility functions but active and creative, the exercise of
the free and creative and (some of us think) God-given
will that can say yes, or no."*

- Deirdre N. McCloskey

Embedded in human action, because it reflects the image of the
Creator, is creativity and freedom. This transcends the robotic
and instinctive reactions that are needed for us to function and
adds a dimension that not only feeds economic life but also feeds
our souls.

"Creativity is the foundation of wealth. All progress comes from the creative minority. Under capitalism, wealth is less a stock of goods than a flow of ideas, the defining characteristic of which is surprise. If it were not surprising, we could plan it, and socialism would work

- George Gilder

Human action always includes surprise. This is true in the very nature of things. This element of surprise is not only where human creativity can shine, but it is a large part of the doomed-to-fail nature of collectivism. Deep central planning cannot take into account the creative capacity of human beings; it will always play catch-up.

"Markets are not just about the steam engine, iron found-ries, or today's silicon-chip factories. Markets also supported Shakespeare, Haydn, and the modern book superstore. The rise of oil painting, classical music, and print culture were all part of the same broad social and economic developments, namely the rise of capitalism, modern technology, rule of law, and consumer society."

- Tyler Cowen

This point is not made enough when we describe the fruits of the free enterprise tree, and that is because those who hold markets in contempt have every objective of "commercializing" enterprise as something sinister. When economics are more rightly viewed as the outpouring of human action, we see a much more holistic picture—that which is consumerist and yes, that which is beautiful, all from the same system and support mechanism.

"Thus there are no 'solutions' in the tragic vision, but only trade-offs that still leave many desires unfulfilled and much unhappiness in the world. What is needed in this vision is a prudent sense of how to make the best trade-offs from the limited options available, and a realization that 'unmet needs' will necessarily remain—that attempting to fully meet these needs seriatim only deprives other people of other things, so that a society pursuing such a policy is like a dog chasing its tail."

- Thomas Sowell

There is no free lunch. Economics is the decision-making process embedded in human action. We price in risks and weight them against hopeful rewards, and we do this with remarkable efficiency. We may mis-gauge a certain risk and find ourselves on the wrong side of a risk-reward trade-off, but that is the essence of economics. Trade-offs are not bad things—they are a fact of life. The only time trade-offs become unbearable is when we deny their basic inevitability to begin with.

COVET-OUSNESS & CLASS ENVY

"Despite those who equate free-market economics with 'greed,' the heyday of laissez-faire economics in the 19th century also saw an unprecedented outpouring of private philanthropy. Moreover the 'materialistic' Americans are unique in the many academic, medical and other institutions founded and sustained with private, voluntary contributions."

- Thomas Sowell

For the camp who advocate social justice via confiscation, this basic fact that Sowell affirms may not be sufficient. Nevertheless, one undeniable by-product of the last 150 years of wealth creation via market forces has been a level of private, voluntary, and therefore charitable endeavors, never before seen in human history. Were the charitable impulses new? Of course not. What was new was the wealth that free enterprise created, which was now available to fund such philanthropic passions.

"The farmer and manufacturer can no more live without profit than the labourer without wages."

- David Ricardo

It is a good thing that we do not look at the worker who demands to be paid for his work and decry him or her as greedy. But when we decry the business owner for pursuing profits, are we not doing the exact same thing? Profits are to the entrepreneur what wages are to the worker. Now, there are some who would say, "allow the entrepreneur to profit, just not too much..." Besides the obvious phariseeism of this thought-process, it also invites tyranny, subjectivity, disincentives, and distortions. Incomes are a noble thing, whether they be received by a worker or an owner and called "profits."

"At least in the United States, most economic resentment is not directed toward billionaires or high-roller financiers—not even corrupt ones. It's directed at the guy down the hall who got a bigger raise. It's directed at the husband of your wife's sister, because he earns 20 percent more than you do."

- Tyler Cowen

How true and tragic this is! Covetousness is a heart issue, and it reveals itself far more in individual relationships and local community attitudes than it even does in one's disdain for Great Gatsby-like opulence. It is not remedied by your friend having his pay cut, but it is also not remedied by your pay going higher. It is remedied by your faithful obedience to the commandment, "Thou shalt not covet." A focus on your own productivity, gratitude for your own bounty, and genuine admiration for the achievement of others—only these things will purge the covetousness that is so incredibly corrosive to our economic culture.

> *"It seems to be almost a law of human nature that it is easier for people to agree on a negative program—on the hatred of an enemy, on the envy of those better off— than on any positive task. The contrast between the 'we' and the 'they,' the common fight against those outside the group, seems to be an essential ingredient in any creed which will solidly knit together a group for common action.... From their point of view it has the great advantage of leaving them greater freedom of action than almost any positive program."*
>
> *- F.A. Hayek*

Covetousness not only carries the emotional gratification of resenting someone else, but it seeks to relieve one's self of the burdens and responsibilities of action. For that reason, it is a double sin. It contains all the corrosive elements of disdaining others for their success while simultaneously preventing us from being our best selves.

"Once financiers are perceived to be socially useless scavengers, it's just a short but critical additional step to label them criminals. With this step, financiers are total delegitimized and there are no limits to what the state can do to them. They are not even entitled to their liberty. Criminalization is also popular with the public because it cloaks envy with self-respect."

- Daniel Fischel

The context of Fischel's quote here is the monstrosity of the Michael Milken arrest in the late 1980s. However, the broader point he makes is incredibly important: Those opposed to the pursuit of wealth and prosperity through free markets will always turn their guns on financial markets eventually. And the way to undermine financial markets is to undermine financiers. And the way to undermine financiers has been to play to the envy of the public by labeling financiers as criminals. It is a clever, but all together wicked, tactic.

"To clear, cultivate, and transform the huge uninhabited continent which is their domain, the Americans need the support of an energetic passion; that passion can only be the love of wealth. So no stigma attaches to the love of money in America, and provided it does not exceed the bounds imposed by public order, it is held in honor."
- *Alexis de Tocqueville*

It would be easy to take this out of context if one does not have at least a surface level familiarity with the great de Tocqueville. What is being celebrated is not an idolatrous love of money (quite the contrary), but rather the world-transforming uniqueness of American aspiration. The pursuit of a higher quality of life and pursuit of happiness, in no way divorced from the transcendent truths and moral requirements of man as created beings, removed from the burden and falsity of guilt, sit at the foundation of American exceptionalism.

"Nor during the Age of Innovation have the poor gotten poorer, as people are always saying. On the contrary, the poor have been the chief beneficiaries of modern capitalism. It is an irrefutable historical finding, obscured by the logical truth that the profits from innovation go in the first act mostly to the bourgeois rich."
- Deirdre N. McCloskey

The sequence of events here is important. The rich do historically profit, first, from new innovations. This reflects a logical and entirely non-controversial fact—that the creators of innovations and those most engaged in the use of the tools that are themselves being innovated feel the benefits most in the initial phase. But that the benefits of free enterprise by degree include the poor is a fact so evident in history, it is only a lack of care for proportion that would disguise this fact. The change in quality of life for the rich may be bothersome to our covetous spirits, but that does not change the fact that systemically, free markets have made the poor exponentially less poor. And we should thank God for this!

"Economics is haunted by more fallacies than any other study known to man. This is no accident. The inherent difficulties of the subject would be great enough in any case, but they are multiplied a thousandfold by a factor that is insignificant in, say, physics, mathematics or medicine—the special pleading of selfish interests."

- *Henry Hazlitt*

This may be the best explanation as to why economics seems to be so much more vulnerable to error than all the other academic disciplines. Not only is economics wrongly viewed as a data science in contemporary times, thereby losing its integral connection to human action; but economics is exponentially more susceptible to the manipulation of special interests who would bastardize it in a second for crony ends. I am sure all disciplines are subject to some degree of this, but none have quite the monetary stakes that nefarious actors would extract from the subject of economics.

"Let me offer you my definition of social justice: I keep what I earn and you keep what you earn. Do you disagree? Well then tell me how much of what I earn belongs to you—and why."

- Walter Williams

The real principle being advocated for here by the great Walter Williams is that of private property and the inherent justice in protecting private property. Systems of confiscation undermine justice. For Williams, social justice starts with the premise of protecting the fruits of one's labor, and then it works from there into discussions of how to fund government, charity, etc. The modern social justice movement does it in reverse. They start with the premise that the fruits of one's labor first belong to the social needs of society, then work into what may be left for the earner or laborer. Social justice is a topic in need of extensive treatment, as it is a loaded term, one with great emotional impact, but one that is never used without strong presuppositions. Unpacking those presuppositions—the ideological commitments one brings to the use of the term—must be our priority.

"[There is] a strange split in thinking common to those on the religious left, who are quick to denounce the profit motive and commercialism. Yet, they seem to think that the key to happiness is giving people more stuff—by enlisting the coercive power of government. This perverse way of thinking holds that 'social justice' demands that we take money from those who have earned it and give it to those who have less of it. That's not social justice; that's materialism."

- Father Robert Sirico

This ought to be one of the primary arguments of defenders of a market economy: That our system seeks to create more fulfilled humans through a process of earned success; and the contrary systems are materialistic to the core. One system is focused on human achievement and flourishing; the other wants to merely give physical things to someone.

"I have never understood why it is 'greed' to want to keep the money you have earned but not greed to want to take somebody else's money."

- Thomas Sowell

This is the irony of the political rhetoric that saturates modern economic discussion. The never-ending ring of voices decrying "greed" are always doing so from a posture of wanting to take what belongs to someone else. We have turned basic definitions on their head.

"Nothing is more usual, among states which have made some advances in commerce, than to look on the progress of their neighbours with a suspicious eye, to consider all trading states as their rivals, and to suppose that it is impossible for any of them to flourish, but at their expense. In opposition to this narrow and malignant opinion, I will venture to assert, that the encrease of riches and commerce in any one nation, instead of hurting, commonly promotes the riches and commerce of all its neighbours; and that a state can scarcely carry its trade and industry very far, where all the surrounding states are buried in ignorance, sloth, and barbarism."

- David Hume

It is not rich countries that hurt poor countries, but poor countries that hurt rich countries, according to the great enlightenment philosopher. His reasoning? The economic treasure of a flourishing country inevitably spills over into neighboring countries, whereas the shortcomings of a country limits the trade and capacity of its neighboring countries. Indeed, this has been evident throughout modern history that prosperous countries are a benefit to their continental neighbors, and weak ones are an albatross to theirs.

"The envy of excellence leads to perdition; the love of it leads to the light."

- George Gilder

Rooted in today's prevalent economic ideology of resentment is the envy of excellence that is divorced from a love of it. Imagine the economic opportunity that opens up when envy is replaced with love, and resentment replaced with admiration. This is not merely a spiritual reality for the person entrapped in covetousness, but it is an economic promise for the system at-large.

"The whole gospel of Karl Marx can be summed up in a single sentence: Hate the man who is better off than you are. Never under any circumstances admit that his success may be due to his own efforts, to the productive contribution he has made to the whole community. Always attribute his success to the exploitation, the cheating, the more or less open robbery of others. Never under any circumstances admit that your own failure may be owing to your own weakness, or that the failure of anyone else may be due to his own defects—his laziness, incompetence, improvidence, or stupidity."

- Henry Hazlitt

Marxism is, at its core, a theology of oppression—the belief that history is the story of a victim and a victimizer. It must first start with a demonization of who will fit this role of victimizer, and to do that, the achievements of the successful must be reduced to sinisterism. But just as much as fantasy is needed to create this oppressor, so is fantasy needed to create the permanently oppressed.

"All of the criticisms one might mount against the corporate form—some of which are valid—pale in contrast to two straightforward and indeed essential virtues. First, business makes most of the stuff we enjoy and consume. Second, business is what gives most of us jobs. The two words that follow most immediately from the world of business are 'prosperity' and 'opportunity.'"

- Tyler Cowen

The contempt too many show for the concept of "business" can only be attributed to a covetous disdain for success. Business as the producer of our purchase habits is inherently true. And business as the place where jobs and opportunity are found is tautologically true. This leaves few logical options for why business is so often said as if it were a four-letter word.

*"That businesspeople buy low and sell high in a partic-
ularly alert and advantageous way does not make them
bad unless all trading is bad, unless when you yourself
shop prudently you are bad, unless any tall poppy needs
to be cut down, unless we wish to run our ethical lives
on the sin of envy."*

- Deirdre N. McCloskey

This should be the most self-evident of statements, but because
of the politics of envy that drives so much of modern economics,
it is not. The transactions of successful business people are not
"evil" when they are profitable, any more than our own endeavors in transacting in the marketplace become suddenly noble
when done foolishly, or suddenly evil when done effectively.
The derogatory way that so many speak of business success
reveals an entire ecosystem of envy.

THE KNOWLEDGE PROBLEM

> *"Dispersed knowledge is essentially dispersed and cannot possibly be gathered together and conveyed to an authority charged with the task of deliberately creating order."*
>
> *- F.A. Hayek*

While Hayek's contributions to 20th century thought should never be limited to merely one quote, it is perhaps this basic notion of "the knowledge problem" that defines Hayekian thought at its finest. Building off of the Misesian notion of human action, Hayek here says, essentially, that no central authority could ever gather the knowledge that is dispersed throughout society in individuals adequately enough to maintain order, let alone optimize prosperity. This basic reality of knowledge undermines the entire thesis of statism and should never be forgotten for any who desire a free and prosperous society.

"At the heart of capitalism is the unification of knowledge and power.... Because knowledge is dispersed, power must be as well."

- George Gilder

Here, Gilder simply applies the brilliance of Hayek's knowledge problem in the most succinct possible way. Trying to centralize knowledge, as the collectivist does, creates horrifically sub-optimal economic outcomes. Trying to centralize power, though, creates destruction.

> *"There is only one difference between a bad economist and a good one: the bad economist confines himself to the visible effect; the good economist takes into account both the effect that can be seen and those effects that must be foreseen."*
>
> - Frédéric Bastiat

When I first began studying economics as a very young man, this quote had a transformative effect on me. It is a rather famous quote, so I am not alone in that. But like the "broken window fallacy" that Bastiat postulated as the preface to this quote, we see that good economics is fundamentally being willing to look beyond the superficial. Bad policies can seem good and good policies can seem bad. It is transcending the readily apparent, the short term, and the easily visible that separates cogent economic policy from the pedestrian and even dangerous.

"The art of economics consists in looking not merely at the immediate but at the longer effects of any act or policy; it consists in tracing the consequences of that policy not merely for one group but for all groups."

- *Henry Hazlitt*

Astute readers will note that this sentiment is nearly identical to what Bastiat communicated in the preceding entry. Hazlitt here elaborated on Bastiat's 19th century work to popularize the "broken window fallacy" and provide a framework for how we understand all misguided economic thinking.

"It is because freedom means the renunciation of direct control of individual efforts that a free society can make use of so much more knowledge than the mind of the wisest ruler could comprehend."

- F.A. Hayek

You may want to read this one several times to let it sink in. In a free society, the collective knowledge of all the individuals in it is at use—it is not suppressed, it has distributive powers, and its applications are monumental and miraculous. The conscious decision to replace the power of that collective knowledge expressed in a free and open marketplace with the limited, broken, misapplied, and misaligned knowledge of a central planner is one of the great mysteries of modern times, and one of its great iniquities.

"The most basic question is not what is best, but who shall decide what is best."

- Thomas Sowell

This is, indeed, the question. Defenders of free enterprise do not believe in a perfect administration under a market economy. Rather, we do not believe in the possibility of such. To the extent imperfect decision-making is accepted, we then seek to solve for who has the best chance of answering the question correctly, he with local knowledge or he without? He who will reap the consequences of his decision, or he who will not? Better decisions that are imperfect are superior to worse ones that are also imperfect. And accountability where a decision is made is better than no accountability where a decision is also made. One simply must abandon belief in the omnipotent disinterested third party (which no one explicitly believes in but too many implicitly do). Once we have accepted the inevitability of imperfect decision-making, choosing who decides is the easy part.

"The Universe is full of dots. Connect the right ones and you can draw anything. The important question is not whether the dots you picked are really there, but why you chose to ignore all the others."

- Russ Roberts

One of the most profound insights in the books! Standing in the way of the knowledge that may enable authoritarians to command the affairs of society is not nearly the lack of basic information, but also the inability to discern what they do see. The knowledge problem extends to what cannot be known and what cannot be understood in proper context from what is seen.

"The curious task of economics is to demonstrate to men how little they really know about what they imagine they can design. To the naive mind that can conceive of order only as the product of deliberate arrangement, it may seem absurd that in complex conditions order, and adaptation to the unknown, can be achieved more effectively by decentralizing decisions and that a division of authority will actually extend the possibility of overall order. Yet that decentralization actually leads to more information being taken into account."

- F.A. Hayek

The irony must not be lost on us. Those who not only do not claim to have adequate knowledge in the details of what they seek to control, but demonstrate their ignorance and inadequacy consistently for all to see, are the loudest proponents of granting the authority to control economic affairs to disinterested third parties. And perhaps I am too focused on their disinterest, the lack of skin in the game, alignment, incentive, and knowledge, and not focused enough on the lack of competence? Choose your poison.

"I prefer true but imperfect knowledge, even if it leaves much undetermined and unpredictable, to a pretense of exact knowledge that is likely to be false."

- F.A. Hayek

No perfect knowledge is possible in the comprehensive sense on this side of glory. And yet individuals operating with freedom and agency do not assert exact knowledge and can freely operate within the constraints of what they know they do not know. Central authorities asserting decision-making control presupposes knowledge they do not have, and worse, make us suffer the consequences where they are wrong.

"In the realm of public policy it is important to insist that principle be upheld in the face of expediency. Arguments for expediency understate the true cost of public policy because they neglect the beneficial outcomes of what would have occurred under a general principle of freedom. The proposed benefits of the expedient path are concrete, but the costs are unseen."

- Peter J. Boettke

A failure to appreciate the knowledge problem allows expediency to take over and promotes policymakers doing what is easy and palatable versus what is right. Unseen costs are ignored (because to analyze or discover them would be hard), but they are inevitable because of the knowledge problem. This dilemma is inescapable when power and control are given to those whom lack the knowledge and vested interest to put the hard over the easy.

"There is beyond question a body of very important but unorganized knowledge which cannot possibly be called scientific in the sense of knowledge of general rules: the knowledge of the particular circumstances of time and place. It is with respect to this that practically every individual has some advantage over all others because he possesses unique information of which beneficial use might be made, but of which use can be made only if the decisions depending on it are left to him or are made with his active cooperation."

- F.A. Hayek

We are really drilling into the knowledge problem here—and that is the particularity of knowledge that is necessary in economic management. Only individuals can possess the unique information which offers context and color to a decision they make. A centrally made decision that lacks such particular context is wholly inadequate and inferior. It would take almost no effort at all for us to imagine the plethora of ways in which individuals know particular things about their own decision tree that cannot be known by those who lack their experience, their surroundings, their particulars of time and place. An economy where those with knowledge act is to be earnestly desired over an economy where decisions are made by know-nothings.

"Probability is not a mere computation of odds on the dice or more complicated variants; it is the acceptance of the lack of certainty in our knowledge and the development of methods for dealing with our ignorance."

- Nassim Taleb

Individuals have an ability to deal with what they do not know more proficiently than does a disinterested third party acting on behalf of a whole population. The "skin in the game" of an individual gives different motives, different processes, and a different awareness to what they do not know in any given situation. In this sense, the knowledge problem is compounded far beyond how the term is generally used. The knowledge problem is not just that a collective cannot know what individuals do know in their local and specific context; it is further that individuals are better equipped to process and mitigate the risk of what can't be known than a collective actor ever could be.

"The case for individual freedom rests chiefly on the recognition of the inevitable and universal ignorance of all of us concerning a great many of the factors on which the achievement of our ends and welfare depend. It is because every individual knows so little and, in particular, because we rarely know which of us knows best that we trust the independent and competitive efforts of many to induce the emergence of what we shall want when we see it. Humiliating to human pride as it may be, we must recognize that the advance and even the preservation of civilization are dependent upon a maximum of opportunity for accidents to happen."

- *F.A. Hayek*

The benefits that come to all of us individually out of the combined wisdom of the market is, itself, a miracle of the market. The state lacks the independence or competitive drivers to produce or facilitate production of what betters the society. And so does any one individual. But the marketplace as a whole, possessing the dispersed knowledge of individuals, operated with freedom and competitive drivers, unleashes the innovations that have made our lives better, time and time again.

"The recognition of the insuperable limits to his knowledge ought indeed to teach the student of society a lesson of humility which should guard him against becoming an accomplice in men's fatal striving to control society—a striving which makes him not only a tyrant over his fellows, but which may well make him the destroyer of a civilization which no brain has designed but which has grown from the free efforts of millions of individuals."

- F.A. Hayek

Tyranny and destruction await the civilization which has given control over itself to that which lacks the knowledge to control it and yet does not know that it lacks such. Freedom and prosperity await the civilization which unleashes the knowledge and effort embedded in human action.

VALUE & PRICE DISCOV-ERY

"Prices are important not because money is considered paramount but because prices are a fast and effective conveyor of information through a vast society in which fragmented knowledge must be coordinated."

  - Thomas Sowell

If we understood prices for what they are—pivotally important signals in a free economy—the last thing we would do is use the coercive power of the state to alter prices. Wage controls, price controls, and artificial manipulation of interest rates all work together to do one thing—vastly distort price discovery in the economy. The results are misinformation delivered to entrepreneurs, a misallocation of resources, and a misunderstanding of risk and reward.

"The creation of wealth is not simply a physical process and cannot be explained by a chain of cause and effect. It is determined not by objective physical facts known to any one mind but by the separate, differing, information of millions, which is precipitated in prices that serve to guide further decisions."

- F.A. Hayek

The complexity of prices is appreciated by the humble and ignored by the arrogant. In the individual prices of goods and services, we receive the best reduction of information readily available to us without the omniscience those who believe themselves qualified to set prices apparently believe they have.

"When I discussed the nature of value, I observed that value is nothing inherent in goods and that it is not a property of goods. But neither is value an independent thing. There is no reason why a good may not have value to one economizing individual but no value to another individual under different circumstances. The measure of value is entirely subjective in nature, and for this reason a good can have great value to one economizing individual, little value to another, and no value at all to a third, depending upon the differences in their requirements and available amount. What one person disdains or values lightly is appreciated by another, and what one person abandons is often picked up by another."

- Carl Menger

The subjective nature of value is philosophically non-negotiable for advocates of a free market economy. Once we have tied value to some objective standard, we have invited an undesirable to the process—the anointed arbiter of that objective value. Subjectivity in value is not only logical and cogent, but necessary to allow exchange to freely occur towards the betterment of all parties.

"Fundamentally, in a system in which the knowledge of the relevant facts is dispersed among many people, prices can act to coordinate the separate actions of different people in the same way as subjective values help the individual to coordinate the parts of his plan."

- F.A. Hayek

Heavy stuff, right? A simple summary may be as follows: We can't see all the knowledge of all people on one screen or in one place, but we can see a price, which reflects that collective knowledge into one place. Value can be subjective, but prices reflect the sum total of knowledge. To distort price discovery is to cut us off from knowledge—from that information which guides the decisions of economic actors. Thus it can be said that price discovery is the *sine qua non* of economic freedom and economic efficiency. Mess with it at your own peril!

"Demand and supply are the opposite extremes of the beam, whence depend the scales of dearness and cheapness; the price is the point of equilibrium, where the momentum of the one ceases, and that of the other begins."

- Jean-Baptiste Say

The economic law of supply and demand, and how price discovery comes out of these two variables, could not possibly be explained more succinctly and eloquently than this. Never static, prices come where supply and demand meet, and immediately move from there as both variables inevitably stay in constant flux.

"There is no necessary and direct connection between the value of a good and whether, or in what quantities, labor and other goods of higher order were applied to its production. A non-economic good (a quantity of timber in a virgin forest, for example) does not attain value for men [since] large quantities of labor or other economic goods were not applied to its production. Whether a diamond was found accidentally or was obtained from a diamond pit with the employment of a thousand days of labor is completely irrelevant for its value. In general, no one in practical life asks for the history of the origin of a good in estimating its value, but considers solely the services that the good will render him and which he would have to forgo if he did not have it at his command.... The quantities of labor or of other means of production applied to its production cannot, therefore, be the determining factor in the value of a good. Comparison of the value of a good with the value of the means of production employed in its production does, of course, show whether and to what extent its production, an act of past human activity, was appropriate or economic. But the quantities of goods employed in the production of a good have neither a necessary nor a directly determining influence on its value."

- Carl Menger

I know this is a mouthful of a quote, and from no less than the founder of Austrian economics. But because of the value the defender of free markets must place on price discovery, it is imperative that Marx's labor theory of value be thoroughly debunked in your minds, and Menger here has made minced meat of this pivotal piece of Marxist thought. Goods (and ser-vices for that matter) contain value to the degree that they will do good for the user of the good or service. Price signals indicate such a measurement of that value. Marxist machinations of how value is defined lead to a slippery slope that distort everything they touch. Price discovery in free enterprise is instrumental in unpacking value.

"In order to understand the movement of prices, you need not an oscilloscope to measure the entire market and reduce it to noise, but a microscope to investigate the creative process behind every company and its price."

- George Gilder

Bottom-up processes, decisions, and circumstances dictate prices, and in this sense, prices are the single most decentralizing force in society. Top-down dictates can impact prices (note the sales tax level in some states vs. others) yet cannot overcome the millions of microscopic complexities that cause such diversity and creativity in prices. The purer the process of price discovery, the greater the signal in the marketplace from which additional economic decisions are made.

SELF – INTER – EST

"It is not from the benevolence of the butcher, the brewer, or the baker that we expect our dinner, but from their regard to their own self-interest. We address ourselves, not to their humanity but to their self-love, and never talk to them of our own necessities but of their advantages."

- Adam Smith

In this widely-quoted excerpt from the great moral philosopher, Adam Smith, a key reality of market economics is borne—the benefits people in society receive from others acting in their own self-interest. This concept is the root of the "profit motive," and it represents so much of the miracle of free enterprise. We cannot benefit ourselves without benefiting others—people will not pay us for goods or services they do not want or need. Out of this doctrine comes mutual cooperation, free exchange, and ultimately, wealth creation. It is the miracle of free enterprise.

"Profit is an inescapable category of human action—all action aims at profit. Any act I perform—from reading a book to digging a hole to blinking my eyes—implies an expectation to substitute a more satisfactory state of affairs for a less satisfactory state. Why else would I act? To criticize broadly 'the desire to profit' is to misconceive the impetus to do anything at all whatsoever.

But profit is in no way limited to material gain, nor to narrow self-interest. People are free to assume the interests of others as their own, and to act on behalf of spiritual ideas. And yet neither case diminishes the expectation to gain from what one is doing."

- Matthew Summers

The entire discussion of economics would be substantially improved if this basic concept was fully understood and allowed to replace the constant, loaded refrain about "profits." One may choose for either ignorant purposes or agendized ones to "financialize" our understanding of profits, but if we understand human action, we understand "profits" in the fully economic sense— the behavioral, the psychological, the charitable, the altruistic, the drive for self-advancement—all together, the cause of the human spirit.

"The fact that our self-regard finds expression in a desire for approval offers an opening for moral education—for moderating both our passions and our animal appetites to make civilized life possible…. [This] is the beginning of social order and of self-restraint, and so the first impulse to moral conformity and common social norms."

- Yuval Levin

The requirement of a moral landscape in an open economy is, unfortunately, at odds with the reality of fallen human nature. And yet, norms, institutions, and traits exist that can, all at once, benefit from man's moral advancement and facilitate more of the same. The moderation of sinful instincts not only creates greater communion for man with God, but it makes possible the social order in which virtue can lead to prosperity.

"The disdain of profit is due to ignorance, and to an attitude that we may if we wish admire in the ascetic who has chosen to be content with a small share of the riches of this world, but which, when actualized in the form of restrictions on profits of others, is selfish to the extent that it imposes asceticism, and indeed deprivations of all sorts, on others."

- F.A. Hayek

It should always strike us as painfully odd that those who claim to reject the profit motive, who claim to strive for material humility, who claim to prize the beautiful over the opulent, would be so audacious as to apply their self-imposed "preferences" on others. There is nothing noble or righteous about imposing on others the virtue-signaling you have chosen for yourself.

> *"All people, however fanatical they may be in their zeal to disparage and to fight capitalism, implicitly pay homage to it by passionately clamoring for the products it turns out."*
>
> *- Ludwig Von Mises*

Oh the irony! But so true, indeed. The modern caricature is especially comical, as some hipster drinking a specialty drink at an artisan coffee shop uses an $800 smart phone to broadcast via a $600 billion social media outlet the great evils of free enterprise and moral superiority of socialism.

"Capitalism is identical with the restraint, or at least a rational tempering, of this irrational impulse. But capitalism is identical with the pursuit of profit, and forever renewed profit, by means of continuous, rational, capitalistic enterprise."

- Max Weber

There is no denying the pursuit of profit—of self-interest—at the heart of free enterprise (though self-interest entails much more than financial profits in a free and virtuous society). But what also must not be denied is that in one's pursuit of such self-interest, a pursuit so wrongly condemned by the envious or misguided, are the very mechanisms needed to moderate and civilize impulses. Further, that pursuit of self-interest succeeds with tenacity and thoughtfulness, not laziness and apathy.

"[The rich] consume little more than the poor, and in spite of their natural selfishness and rapacity...they divide with the poor the produce of all their improvements. They are led by an invisible hand to make nearly the same distribution of the necessaries of life, which would have been made, had the earth been divided into equal portions among all its inhabitants, and thus without intending it, without knowing it, advance the interest of the society, and afford means to the multiplication of the species."

- Adam Smith

The sinful nature of man cannot be lost on those of us defending free enterprise. Our case is not that mankind's fall is suspended when he transacts in the marketplace; it is that the marketplace best tames our fallen nature. Our case is not that collective well-being is more important to the entrepreneur than his or her individual well-being; it is that what is best for the individual is most connected to what is best for the collective in a market economy. A public life that is oriented around free exchange between producers and consumers will create a far more cooperative and mutually beneficial result than any alternative ever considered in the annals of history.

"A successful economy depends on the proliferation of the rich, on creating a large class of risk-taking men who are willing to shun the easy channels of a comfortable life in order to create new enterprise, win huge profits, and invest them again."

- *George Gilder*

For all of the talk about self-interest in what it means for the economic system and where the potential for a virtuous cycle lies, we must never forget that even beyond the "profit motive" and "self-interest" (phrases that are easily migrated into the unseemly and pejorative) is "risk-taking." Those acting in self-interest do not have access to a free lunch, either. Not only does the profit motive lead to all sorts of economic benefit, but it requires the actor in pursuit of it to take risk and make sacrifices. This perspective ought to soften the demonization of the profit-seeking actor, especially since that demonization is so wrong-headed to begin with.

"How selfish soever man may be supposed, there are evidently some principles in his nature, which interest him in the fortune of others, and render their happiness necessary to him, though he derives nothing from it except the pleasure of seeing it."

- Adam Smith

The simplistic notion that self-interest is only monetary, only materialistic, only crass, only opulent—it helps feed a narrative that is useful to the cause of class envy. But it ignores the complexity of human nature and the basic fact of those who take pleasure in serving their fellow mankind. Those with such an altruistic intuition, informed by moral conscience and obedience, possess every right to pursue their own material betterment in their pursuits. But for commentators on the drivers of enterprise to assume a pedestrian view of human objective is convenient, dishonest, and ideological. The study of human action shows ample capacity for pleasure derived from service.

"Nothing contributes so much to the prosperity and happiness of a country as high profits."

- David Ricardo

In a market economy, we can look to the profit motive as the driver of success and productivity. And indeed, that outflow of human action in the profit motive (properly understood) is the source of incredible output. But to look at the profits achieved without an understanding of what it means to the nation at large is a colossal failure of economics. Countries where citizens are generating large profits in their individual efforts are countries with a higher tax base, with higher research and development, with better public services, with more robust charity and philanthropy, with greater happiness and quality of life. Such prosperity is distributed far and wide in a market economy.

GOVERNMENT SPENDING & DEBT

"The costs of fiscal irresponsibility have more to do with constraints on future growth and spending than with the risk of catastrophic crisis. Growing debt makes claims on the government's finances in the years to come, and so burdens future taxpayers while limiting the options of future legislators. The problem, in other words, is that debt and interest payments will dramatically constrain the government's capacity for discretionary spending—on defense, on welfare, on research, on emergency response—and will also constrain our economy's capacity for prosperity."

- Yuval Levin

We all intuitively know in our personal financial lives that taking on debt today, especially debt that our cash flow easily enables us to service, is not short term catastrophic. Likewise, the debt the government takes on never feels catastrophic in the short term. Yet that is almost always how we talk about it economically—as if the dam will break tomorrow—when in reality, what excessive debt taken now does most detrimentally is *dramatically hamper our future growth and flexibility*. When future growth gets pulled into the present, it only means one thing: Less growth in the future. We know this when we buy a living room full of new furniture in anticipation of a bonus coming next year (that bonus will now not "grow" our net worth next year). And we know it when the government spends future tax receipts today—the growth and flexibility of the future are handcuffed. This is mathematically and intuitively obvious.

"Everyone wants to live at the expense of the state. They forget that the state lives at the expense of everyone."

- Frédéric Bastiat

Our conversations about government spending would be so dramatically different if we first realized that the government has no money to spend that it does not first take from someone else. Whether it be confiscation (taxation) or debt (future confiscation), government spending, legitimate to the extent that it funds the necessities of government, is always, tautologically, an extraction of wealth from the private sector. All but the anarchists know there is some legitimate necessity for government funding. Once we start with the basic premise I describe herein—that such spending is essentially a conversation about how much money we want to extract from private citizens—we can have a more honest, and hopefully useful, conversation.

"Everything we get, outside of the free gifts of nature, must in some way be paid for. The world is full of so-called economists who in turn are full of schemes for getting something for nothing. They tell us that the government can spend and spend without taxing at all; that it can continue to pile up debt without ever paying it off, because 'we owe it to ourselves.'"

- Henry Hazlitt

There is no free lunch. We can talk about all the things we want accomplished with government spending all day—and indeed, we can always find legitimate expenditures in the government P&L. But the idea that the treasury can spend infinite dollars and there will be no consequence is the fundamental, basic, never-ending economic mistake of believing in free lunch. What is the trade-off for excessive government spending? Capital misallocation. Depressed growth. Higher taxes. Less competitive advantage. Some or all of the above. Take your pick. Just don't fall for the belief that there is no trade-off. There is always a trade-off.

"What I'm not saying is that all government spending is bad...but there is no free lunch.... There is no public tooth fairy. Father Christmas does not work on the Treasury staff this year. You can never bail someone out of trouble without putting someone else into trouble."

- Dr. Art Laffer

When he speaks in public, Dr. Laffer does a bit where he asks the audience to pretend the entire world is composed of just two farms, and that one farmer is receiving unemployment benefits. He then states that the other farmer is paying the unemployment benefits, then asks the audience if this is going over their heads. It is always good for a laugh, and yet while we can laugh at the obviousness of his point with only two farms, we seem to miss this entirely when it comes to a populous society. Government spending is, by definition, confiscatory. And government spending is, by definition, redistributionist. And there are some legitimate expenses in government! But to fail to understand the cost of lunch—the trade-off—is to leave ourselves susceptible to the worst kind of applied economics.

"Nothing is so permanent as a temporary government program."

- Milton Friedman

Our understanding of government spending will go a long way if we first understand this—passing new spending bills in Congress has one level of difficulty; getting rid of some spending program is almost an impossibility. The reason is entrenched in the reality of government programs themselves. Once a program is passed, there is someone, somewhere, living off the benefits of "other people's money." Bureaucrats, lobbyists, other seedy characters—yes. But also, constituents. Voting constituents. Government programs by definition, in one form or another, involve a transfer of funds from one party to another party. That second party—the recipient—has no interest in letting that end and is perfectly capable of building an apparatus that will make it nearly impossible to end.

"For 250 years of American history, politicians have held the peacetime budget deficit in check because of fears of either inflation or higher interest rates (or perhaps a loss of confidence in the gold standard.) What would happen if they begin to sniff out that the actual risk is not inflation or much higher interest rates next year, rather the risk is higher taxes in 20 years, after they've safely retired? How would they respond to this information?"

- Scott Sumner

The incredible point the provocative and insightful Sumner makes here is that so many have focused on the threat of inflation as a way of scaring the public around government spending. From the mid-1980s through present times, inflation has stayed reasonably contained in a broad level and certainly interest rates have embarked upon a forty-year decline. Lo and behold, as the doom and gloom of rising inflation and rising interest rates has proven misguided, so has the public's apathy about government spending. But that excessive debt does have a cost! Getting the cost right is imperative if we are to make clear there is no free lunch. Higher taxes and lower growth—that is the price to be paid for runaway government.

"There are men regarded today as brilliant economists, who deprecate saving and recommend squandering on a national scale as the way of economic salvation; and when anyone points to what the consequences of these policies will be in the long run, they reply flippantly, as might the prodigal son of a warning father: 'In the long run we are all dead.' And such shallow wisecracks pass as devastating epigrams and the ripest wisdom."

- Henry Hazlitt

Hazlitt has in his crosshairs here, of course, John Maynard Keynes. The proper allocation of resources in a society can never treat saving as an evil, for without saving there is no investment; and without investment, there is no future. Likewise, a proper stewardship of resources can never act as if debt is immaterial in the long run. The only person for who long term debt does not matter is the person who holds his children, grandchildren, and future generations in disdain. For such a person, I have no kind words.

"It is not true that Congress spends money like a drunken sailor. Drunken sailors spend their own money. Congress spends our money."

- Dr. Art Laffer

This may be funny, but it is also true. Profligate spending has a particularly negative connotation with it when it is one's own money. But when extravagant, wasteful, reckless spending *of someone else's money* takes place, it is a double dishonor.

FREE TRADE

"Trade protection accumulates upon a single point the good which it effects, while the evil inflicted is infused throughout the mass. The one strikes the eye at a first glance, while the other becomes perceptible only to close investigation."

- *Frédéric Bastiat*

Herein lies the rub on protectionism—the singular benefit to the single actor it creates is easily identifiable, but the broad and lasting damage it does to a host of actors requires further inquiry. This in no way makes the damage protectionism does any less potent.

*"Peace prevailed, in large part, because non-interven-
tion became the hallmark of foreign policy…. There was
unprecedented freedom of movement for people, goods,
and capital…. Trade expanded, strengthening the stake
that nations had in the continued prosperity of one
another as customers and suppliers. While free trade
was never a guarantee of peace, it reduced the danger
of war more than any public policy ever had."*

- Jim Powell

The last part of this entirely brilliant sentiment, and the nuance
therein, is so important. Countries that trade with each other may
very well not like each other, but the risk of war violence is exponentially reduced. History and common sense tell us this. That
there is no "guarantee" does not give us the right to ignore the
substantial wisdom in risk mitigation such beneficial cooperation affords. All the treaties and policies in human history have
not reduced nation-on-nation violence as much as free trade has.

"*Holding...eternal justice to [include] the inalienable right of every man freely to exchange the result of his labor for the productions of other people, and maintaining the practice of protecting one part of the community at the expense of all other classes to be unsound and unjustifiable...carry out to the fullest extent...the true and peaceful principles of Free Trade, by removing all existing obstacles to the unrestricted employment of industry and capital.*"

- Richard Cobden

Though touchy and even toxic in modern times, Cobden here highlights the real objection to free trade from her critics—a protection of one part of the community at the expense of another. Such "protectionism" has a truly sympathetic appeal and yet economically misses a major point of economics—not judging the wisdom of a policy on how it impacts one group in one short period, but all groups in long periods.

"Complete free trade is not politically feasible. Why? Because it's only in the general interest and in no one's special interest."

- Milton Friedman

Perhaps it is a political statement as much as an economic one, but undoubtedly opposition to free trade comes from connected and particular interests, not the objective interests of the society at large. The domestic company who wants to cut off another domestic company from doing business with an international company is not looking to hurt the international company; they are looking to hurt the other domestic company who is their competitor.

"The message from history is so blatantly obvious—that free trade causes mutual prosperity while protectionism causes poverty—that it seems incredible that anybody ever thinks otherwise. There is not a single example of a country opening its borders to trade and ending up poorer."

- *Matt Ridley*

Modern political and even cultural debate around free trade does not center around its impact to the country opening its borders to it. Even free trade opponents know it will make that country richer. The controversy comes around the "mutual prosperity" that Ridley speaks of, which is to say, the former maker of a good inside country A that country A will now buy from country B. Disenfranchising a company in country A to serve the consumers of country A and benefit the company in country B is alleged to be unfair or immoral for the company in country A. But of course, such protectionism—the notion that the consumers of this country should be hurt with higher prices in order to help a company that would otherwise lose the business—is simply moving the victim in your own country from one person to another. Yes, one is more identifiable than the other, but there is no free lunch here.

The nature of trade agreements between countries warrants ample discussion (and such discussion will be better served once participants understand that countries do not trade with each other, companies trade with each other, presumably under the guidance of what best serves that company's needs). There are legitimate discussions around matters of national security, intellectual property, and supply chain sufficiency for health and welfare. But what cannot be denied in the most basic of senses, if we are to have an intellectually honest discussion about free trade, is that free trade causes mutual prosperity and protectionism causes poverty. To deny that is to deny the most basic reality of market function.

"Love locally, trade globally."
- *Russ Roberts*

Most of us have heard the expression or seen the bumper sticker, "Think globally, act locally." The intent (for some) may be benign, but the meaning is generally that our mindset ought to be on a global betterment, and we ought to do so with local steward-ship that protects global interests (especially the environment). Roberts' twist on the misguided bumper sticker adds exponen-tially more wisdom and practicality. We love most those who are closest to us, and they love us the most in return. Strangers in a strange land cannot love us, because they do not know us. It is an empty platitude to talk about love in a generic and impersonal manner, devoid of relationship, commitment, and sacrifice. And in the second half of Roberts' revision, we get the proper behav-ior for those who actually do want to impact global betterment—the practice of free exchange. Societies benefit one another when they trade with one another, and real love and meaningful rela-tionships happen in our most local of bonds and ties. This is not controversial but has somehow been ignored as we have sought to replace these concepts with bubble-gum ideology that gets both the local and global part wrong.

"The one thing that people overlook is that the sort of dependence that results from exchange, i.e., from commercial transactions, is a reciprocal dependence. We cannot be dependent upon a foreigner without his being dependent upon us. Now, this is what constitutes the very essence of society. To sever natural interrelations is not to make oneself independent, but to isolate oneself completely."

- Frédéric Bastiat

Critics of free trade, properly understood, have always treated the concept as if there were a winner and a loser. We must understand the macro advantages to the producer to open up new markets for consumption, and the advantages to the consumer to benefit from the comparative advantages of broader markets for production.

"The great danger to the consumer is the monopoly—whether private or governmental. His most effective protection is free competition at home and free trade throughout the world. The consumer is protected from being exploited by one seller by the existence of another seller from whom he can buy and who is eager to sell to him. Alternative sources of supply protect the consumer far more effectively than all the Ralph Nader's of the world."

- *Milton Friedman*

Nader was an appropriate target in the context and timing of this writing, but there are countless substitutes available since. At the heart of free trade is not just the lower cost of production for the producer that comparative advantage creates; it is also the benefits to the consumer that lower cost and greater choice represents.

CRONY CAPITALISM

"Crony capitalism is about hollowing-out market economies and replacing them with what may be described as political markets. In political markets, the focus is no longer upon prospering through creating, refining, and offering products and services at competitive prices. Instead, economic success depends upon people's ability to harness government power to stack the economic deck in their favor. While the market's outward form is maintained, its essential workings are supplanted by the struggle to ensure that governments, legislators, and regulators favor you at other people's expense. In that sense, crony capitalism certain constitutes a form of redistribution: away from taxpayers, consumers and business focused on creating wealth, and towards the organized, powerful, and politically-connected."

- Dr. Samuel Gregg

A critique and a comprehensive definition rolled into one, what Dr. Gregg has done here is offer the most simple and fair definitions of crony capitalism, while simultaneously demonstrating the basis for its destructiveness.

"But it [crony capitalism] erodes our overall standard of living and stifles entrepreneurs by rewarding the politically favored rather than those who provide what consumers want."

- Charles G. Koch

It does this in a lot of ways. It misallocates resources. It undermines trust in market mechanisms. It builds cynicism in the society. And it distorts markets away from their natural outcomes. If any of these things are acceptable, than what do we need free markets for at all?

"When the government makes loans or subsidies to business, what it does is to tax successful private business in order to support unsuccessful private business."

- Henry Hazlitt

We must never forget that the mere existence of a benefit the government gives to some favored actor must first be taken from some other. The government does not have a "subsidy tree" or "crony tree" from which they can pick fruit and hand out at their discretion. The government's picking of winners and losers is not an active help to those they want, but neutral to the other party. There is an active move to help one, and an active move to hurt another.

"[Corporations] should be subject to the rules of open competition without exception—rules that will turn their self-interest toward more constructive paths. Otherwise, both the efficiency of the market and the public's confidence in the fairness and legitimacy of the system will be dangerously undercut. Capitalism is a fundamentally populist enterprise governed in the interests of the mass of consumers, and it depends upon a clear separation between government and business. If that line is blurred, many of the benefits of the system—both economic and moral—are badly undermined."

- Yuval Levin

This dual danger is important. Cronyism is a moral iniquity, rewarding the rich and powerful over the less-favored and entrenched. It violates the entire ethic of Biblical exhortations and allows some to throw the baby out with the bathwater. The vast majority of criticisms I have heard of free market systems were, in fact, criticisms of cronyism that shot too far and too wide. We must protect the morality and economic cogency of free enterprise from such frustrated attacks.

"Regulation is useful and proper, when aimed at the pre-vention of fraud or contrivance, manifestly injurious to other kinds of production, or to the public safety, and not at prescribing the nature of the products and the methods of fabrication."

- Jean-Baptiste Say

A perfect criteria is offered to us by the great classical economist here: Let regulation be limited to the prevention of fraud, and not at all to favor one product over another.

"The person who profits from this law will complain bitterly, defending his acquired rights. He will claim that the state is obligated to protect and encourage his particular industry; that this procedure enriches the state because the protected industry is thus able to spend more and to pay higher wages to the poor workingmen. Do not listen to this sophistry by vested interests. The acceptance of these arguments will build legal plunder into a whole system. In fact, this has already occurred. The present-day delusion is an attempt to enrich everyone at the expense of everyone else; to make plunder universal under the pretense of organizing it."

- Frédéric Bastiat

I can only say that the prophetic nature of what Bastiat writes here is borderline creepy. That 21st century defenses of cronyism borrowing from the 19th century pleadings of rent-seekers which Bastiat warned us against over 150 years ago says much about the immutability of human nature and the gravity of what is at stake here.

"Yet each favor and handout and protection of vested interests shifts the direction of capital and labor artificially, resulting in over-investment in, say, mortgaged houses, or an over-investment in corruption."

- Deirdre N. McCloskey

Cronyism is not patently unfair, but it is highly distortive to markets and ultimately leads to mal-investment. We have seen this in unspeakable application with the housing crisis, and yet those who would have the government put their thumbs on the scale of a given sector or industry have in no way been muted.

"As government regulates business more, that favors corporations large enough to have substantial legal and compliance departments. Regulation serves as a kind of fixed cost of doing business, discouraging market entry. Not only do higher rates of regulatory growth correlate with increases in market concentration ratios, but the period during which regulation increased significantly, 1990–2000, was followed by increases in market concentration. None of those correlations prove causality, but at the very least it is possible that government regulation is a major force behind the rise of market power."

- *Tyler Cowen*

Regulation is a subsidy. There is no more cronyist tool in human history than that of regulation. It favors the already big and discourages, if not pulverizes, the aspirational.

"Populist economic proposals are by nature a disorganized grab bag of rent-seeking and opportunism on the part of both politicians and their domestic business clients ... [these proposals] lay a heavier governmental hand on economic activity, protecting politically sensitive businesses and industries even if that means artificially reducing the overall standard of living, curtailing traditional economic rights, and violating the rule of law."

- Kevin Williamson

What collectivism and populism have in common is the tactic of using the state to benefit a targeted party. Asking the state to coerce, manipulate, interfere, interject, obfuscate, and otherwise distort free exchange does not become more noble because the actor asking for it says he speaks for the "little guy" as opposed to the actor speaking for a bureaucratic central body. The intent of the intervention does not alter the intervention, and once one decides that state interventions are a good and healthy thing to systematically command-control the economy, they have become a collectivist, whether or not they dress it up in populist clothing.

"Many businesses with unpopular products or inefficient production find it much easier to curry the favor of a few influential politicians or a government agency than to compete in the open market."

- Charles G. Koch

This is actually the essence of crony capitalism. It rarely starts with a corrupt politician looking for a favored business to support, but almost always starts with a deficient business looking for a corrupt politician to aid in its own corruption. Such alliances are easier to form than business savvy is to develop. And often, the use of government and rent-seeking to stifle competition is itself considered its own savvy, and it is confused for real enterprise and competitive advantage.

"If our own misery pinches us very severely, we have no leisure to attend to that of our neighbor."

- Adam Smith

Prosperity is necessary for a good society in that it allows us the luxury of empathy, sacrifice, and generosity.

"Now, legal plunder can be committed in an infinite number of ways. Thus we have an infinite number of plans for organizing it: tariffs, protection, benefits, subsidies, encouragements, progressive taxation, public schools, guaranteed jobs, guaranteed profits, minimum wages, a right to relief, a right to the tools of labor, free credit, and so on, and so on."

- Frédéric Bastiat

All tools available to the crony capitalist and her accomplice, the politician, have one thing in common: The thumb of government on the scale of markets. That some tools are more subtle than others does not change the fact that such interventions are corrupt when they seek to show favoritism to one economic actor over another. Legal plunder, indeed!

"Again, the main issue is not control-seeking bosses versus freedom-seeking workers; very often the person most likely to restrict the workplace freedom of one worker is another worker."

- Tyler Cowen

Indeed, the saddest examples of crony capitalism come today from those on an even playing field, seeking to use leverage, power, and the authority of a disinterested third party to advantage themselves by restricting someone else. Those who resist Right to Work laws are case in point. Cronyism is wrong when it comes from the C-suite, and it is wrong when it comes with the "cause of the laborer" attached to it.

"Properly understood, the case for capitalism is not a case for license or for laissez faire. It is a case for national wealth as a moral good; for the interest of the mass of consumers as the guide of policy; for clear and uniform rules of competition imposed upon all; for letting markets set prices, letting buyers make choices, and letting producers experiment, innovate, and make what they think they can sell—all while protecting consumers and punishing abuses. It is a case for avoiding concentrations of power, for keeping business and government separate, and for letting those who can meet their own needs do so. It is a case for humility about our ability to know, and therefore about our capacity to do."

- Yuval Levin

Each of the moral aspirations we hope for about our society, and each of the economic objectives we have in a free enterprise economy, are undermined by an overly cozy relationship with business and government, where the coercive power of the state is allowed to pick winners and losers. Our case for a market economy is a noble one, but it is undermined from start to finish when we fail to condemn the insidious effects of crony capitalism.

"Nothing is more deadly to achievement than the belief that effort will not be rewarded, that the world is a bleak and discriminatory place in which only the predatory and the specially preferred can get ahead."

- George Gilder

How cronyism can destroy the human spirit and create extreme cynicism is perhaps its worst component. Human action is a powerful force, and human inaction equally so. When one believes the game is rigged, inactivity results. Cronyism strikes at the incentives of free enterprise and robs the would-be economic actor of aspiration. In this sense, cronyism joins collectivism as the primary enemy of a free and virtuous society.

"Sometimes the law defends plunder and participates in it. Thus the beneficiaries are spared the shame and danger that their acts would otherwise involve... But how is this legal plunder to be identified? Quite simply. See if the law takes from some persons what belongs to them and gives it to the other persons to whom it doesn't belong. See if the law benefits one citizen at the expense of another by doing what the citizen himself cannot do without committing a crime. Then abolish that law without delay—no legal plunder; this is the principle of justice, peace, order, stability, harmony and logic."

- Frédéric Bastiat

The principles of identifying and shunning plunder (crony capitalism and corruption) identified by the great Bastiat seem positively naïve in today's economy. What should have been abolished in Bastiat's day by this perfectly moral standard is almost par for the course in so much of today's accepted systems. The manipulation of the tax system to punish one actor and benefit another is plunder. The use of the regulatory system to do the same is plunder. Note what is at stake, here—justice, peace, order, stability—when the people believe the system and the law itself are used to benefit one favored participant over another, the very peace and harmony of social order break down. No defender of free enterprise can ever let the war against crony capitalism become a secondary concern. It is the very fight for free enterprise, itself.

MINI-
MUM
WAGE

"The real problem is that workers are not so much underpaid as they are under-skilled. And the real task is to help those people become skilled. Congress cannot do this simply by declaring that as of such-and-such a date, everybody's productive output is now worth $7.25 per hour [or $15, hour –DLB]. This makes about as much sense, and does just about as much harm, as doctors 'curing' patients simply by declaring that they are cured."

- Walter Williams

If everyone in the minimum wage policy debate could absorb this message, the entire debate could go away. We don't lose weight by altering our scales. And we don't solve for the value of output (the price of wages) by declaring the value to be higher. We solve for output—that is, the value of the productivity. If the same effort went into cultivating the skills of our workforce as goes into altering the free exchange involved labor transactions, we could end this controversy once and for all.

"Only if we understand why and how certain kinds of economic controls tend to paralyze the driving forces of a free society, and which kinds of measures are particularly dangerous in this respect, can we hope that social experimentation will not lead us into situations none of us want."

- F.A. Hayek

While Hayek was clearly writing about a much broader policy apparatus than just the minimum wage law, we certainly see minimum wage setting a tremendous example of what he was warning against. A law that is clearly driven by social experimentation has delivered unintended yet foreseeable consequences that cannot be considered positives for the society at-large.

"You cannot make a man worth a given amount by making it illegal for anyone to offer him anything less. You merely deprive him of the right to earn the amount that his abilities and situation would permit him to earn, while you deprive the community even of the moderate services that he is capable of rendering. In brief, for a low wage you substitute unemployment. You do harm all around, with no comparable compensation."

- Henry Hazlitt

The unintended consequences of this policy aberration are vast—they hurt the would-be worker, they hurt the would-be employer, and they hurt the community at-large.

"Like all other contracts, wages should be left to the fair and free competition of the market, and should never be controlled by the interference of the legislature."

- David Ricardo

What the great classical economist does here is remarkable in its prescience—he notes the similarity between wage manipulation and all other contract price manipulation. Over 150 years later, the concept of government-set contract terms would still be unfathomable in a market economy, yet wage controls by federal government fiat would gain a foothold. Ricardo's warnings are rooted in the consistency of first principles broadly applied—the setting of prices (including the price of wages) is best left to the two parties in the exchange.

"Who bears the burden of the minimum wage? As suggested earlier, it is the workers who are the most marginal, that is, those who employers perceive as being less productive, more costly, or otherwise less desirable to employ than other workers. In the U.S. there are at least two segments of the labor force that share marginal worker characteristics to a greater extent than do other segments of the labor force. The first group consists of youths in general. They are low-skilled or marginal because of their age, immaturity, and lack of work experience. The second group, which contains members of the first, are racial minorities, such as blacks and Hispanics who, as a result of historical factors, are disproportionately represented among low-skilled workers. They are not only made less employable by minimum wages; opportunities to upgrade their skills through on-the-job training are also severely limited when they find it hard to get jobs. It is precisely these labor market participants who are disproportionately represented among the unemployment statistics."

- Walter Williams

Entry level jobs are a wonderful place for teenagers to develop life skills. Minimum wage laws are destroying teenage employment in our country, a cultural development that is almost impossible to understate its malignant effects. Here, Williams also points out the undermining of on-the-job training (and with it, pursuit of mobility) that minimum wage laws create for low-skilled workers.

"Does a merchant increase his sales by raising prices? Does higher pay of domestic servants induce more housewives to hire help? The situation is no different for other employers. The higher wage rate decreed by Congress for low-paid workers will raise the cost of the goods that these workers produce—and must discourage sales. It will also induce employers to replace such workers with other workers—either to do the same work or to produce machinery to do the same work or to produce machinery to do the work."

- Milton Friedman

Leave it to the master to point out the unintended consequence of coerced increase in the cost of labor—a pass-through of that expense to the consumer of what the business provides! To deny this is to deny one of the most basic laws of economics, that the cost of goods is embedded in its price, and that labor is itself a contributor to the cost of goods.

"People who lack the capacity to earn a decent living need to be helped, but they will not be helped by minimum-wage laws, trade-union wage pressures or other devices which seek to compel employers to pay them more than their work is worth. The more likely outcome of such regulations is that the intended beneficiaries are not employed at all."

- James Tobin

Fixing the price of a wage above the value of the work the wage produces results in less workers being hired and no wages being paid to the workers not hired because of this price/value distortion. This is not a partisan notion, and it never has been.

"Many well-meaning people favor legal minimum-wage rates in the mistaken belief that they help the poor. These people confuse wage rates with wage income. It has always been a mystery to me to understand why a youngster is better off unemployed at $1.60 an hour than employed at $1.25."

- Milton Friedman

Our concern should be on the *income* of our labor force, money *actually received* by workers. The *rate* reflects something entirely different than the *income.* Ten people receiving $100 is more income than seven people receiving $120. This is mere math, but it is also pure economics.

"Employer substitution of higher-skilled for lower-skilled workers is not the only effect of the minimum wage law. It also gives employers an economic incentive to make other changes: substitute machines for labor; change production techniques; relocate overseas; and eliminate certain jobs altogether. The substitution of automatic dishwashers for hand washing, and automatic toma-to-picking machines for manual pickers, are examples of the substitution of machines for labor in response to higher wages."

- Walter Williams

We no longer have to postulate as to whether or not this "theory" from Williams is true (it always was self-evident logically). Reality has seen it play out in spades.

> *"The groups that will be hurt the most are the low-paid and the unskilled. The ones who remain employed will receive higher wage rates, but fewer will be employed.... The loss to the unskilled workers will not be offset by gains to others. Smaller total employment will result in a smaller total output. Hence the community as a whole will be worse off."*
>
> - *Milton Friedman*

Lesser employment at a higher wage does not magically create more output. The interest of the society, economically, is in total output. A higher wage for those retained in a government mandate of such does not facilitate higher productivity. Indeed, it is not even intended to do so. It sacrifices total output (the needs of the many) for a higher wage rate (the needs of the few), with no regard for the zero-wage rate paid to the marginalized worker priced out of the equation.

"Nothing should be more obvious than that the business organism cannot function according to design when its most important 'parameters of action'—wages, prices, interest—are transferred to the political sphere and there dealt with according to the requirements of the political game or, which sometimes is more serious still, according to the ideas of some planners."

- Joseph A. Schumpeter

I could have just as easily included this in the "Sound Money" section, for the same principle is at play. The price of money does not belong in the political sphere, and neither does the price of wages. The objectives in that sphere are far different than the objectives in the private sector, and I mean that as negatively as could possibly be.

CREAT-
IVE
DESTRUC-
TION

"Capitalism, then, is by nature a form or method of economic change, and not only never is, but never can be, stationary.... The fundamental impulse that sets and keeps the capitalist engine in motion comes from the new consumers' goods, the new methods of production or transportation, the new markets, the new forms of industrial organization that capitalist enterprise creates."

- Joseph A. Schumpeter

Free enterprise is evolutionary by definition—and if it were not, it would lack the innovation to meet demand. Every variable in the system changes, evolves, and improves—and with these tiers of change comes unimaginable flourishing, and yes, along the way, destruction. That this destruction is necessary for the greater flourishing that flows from it does not negate the reality of short-term pain. But it does give wise men and women pause before intervening!

"Those who favor a 'grand plan' over experimentation fail to understand the role that failed experiments play in creating progress in society. Failures quickly and efficiently signal what doesn't work, minimizing waste and redirecting scarce resources to what does work. A market economy is an experimental discovery process, in which business failures are inevitable and any attempt to eliminate them only ensures even greater failures."

- Charles G. Koch

Markets as recurring discovery processes is a concept I want all readers to fully grasp. I can herald the miracles and achievements of markets all day long, but if I ignore *how* and *why* markets perform this way, I fail in my aim. We must not shy away from the comprehensive story of markets—that in their role as a discovery process, they uncover successes *and failures*. Effective market mechanisms purge those failures, and we are all better for it.

"The essential point to grasp is that in dealing with capitalism we are dealing with an evolutionary process... At the heart of capitalism is creative destruction. Situations emerge in the process of creative destruction in which many firms may have to perish that nevertheless would be able to live on vigorously and usefully if they could weather a particular storm."

- Joseph A. Schumpeter

We hear plenty from the great Schumpeter throughout this book for good reason. But in this quote, we see three things that are all vital to a worldview of free enterprise. One is the ever-changing nature of it—the dynamics of human action, human needs, and human capabilities are always changing, and therefore the manner in which this is manifested in the marketplace is always changing. This inevitably leads to failures and successes, the latter often creating the former. But not all "creative destruction" is the natural result of competitive reality—much of it flows from the inability to survive difficult times. Free enterprise involves offense and defense.

"One of the big reasons why the entrepreneurial spirit flourishes in America is that as a people we seem to be more tolerant of failure. We're taught from little up that if at first you don't succeed, try, try again."

- Jude Wanniski

This is a cultural reality that should not be taken lightly in the United States. We have traditionally loved stories of redemption—stories of overcoming adversity—and there is no story of success more heartwarming than one that started with failure. In societies where early failures are considered sources of shame, they deprive themselves the successful flourishing that comes from the second or third or fourth act. In free enterprise, failure is not just tolerated—more aligning our economic framework to the realities of life—but it is embraced as a necessary ingredient for entrepreneurial success.

"I should regret very much to have you miss the glorious feeling of accomplishment and I know you are not going to let me down. Remember that often adversity is a blessing in disguise and is certainly the greatest character builder."

- Charles G. Koch

What is true of our personal lives is true of the economy—that in overcoming difficulties, we become more resilient, more capable, and more productive. Unless one believes that resilience, capability, and productivity are bad things, we ought to embrace the character and progress that comes from adversity—from transcending failure en route to a more improved outcome.

"Rapid progress is unsettling. Malthus wrote about his very deeply pessimistic economics just at the outset of the industrial revolution when mankind was making this tremendous leap. Well, these leaps of progress cause rapid change, and in rapid change there are always people who lose.... This is a real problem. Reaction comes, then, when we want to stop all this upset and all this tumult and all this change, and there is kind of a societal reaction to slow things down. But you find that when you try to do that, then the whole economy slows down. That, I think, is the paradox."

- Robert L. Bartley

Attempting to soften the impact of targeted disruption in economic progress leads to softening economic progress, always and forever. More people are hurt over a longer period of time when we resist the rapid progress that often happens.

"Failure is part of the natural cycle of business. Companies are born, companies die, capitalism moves forward."

- Thomas Sowell

The biggest mistake one could make is to interpret this sentiment as insensitive to the plight of those who hurt in this process. Nothing could be further from the truth. The creative destruction of a market economy is, all at once, destructive to one group in the short term, while being constructive for all groups in the long term. How does the failure of one business in one moment of time benefit everyone long term? Because if we did not have a system where a business could fail, we would not have a system where any could succeed. And that would mean the death of prosperity and opportunity.

"A policy of subsidizing failures will end in an econ-
omy strewn with capital-guzzling industries long past
their time of profitability—old companies that cannot
create jobs themselves, but can stand in the way of job
creation."

- George Gilder

The reason to understand creative destruction in one's understanding of free enterprise is not merely to enable emotional
acceptance of its necessity, though that is important. The policy tools designed to resist creative destruction are, themselves,
among the most destructive things any free economy has ever
encountered. If we desire job creation, then we cannot support
subsidizing failed companies. Nothing less than optimal resource
allocation is at stake in the subject of creative destruction.

"The opening up of new markets, foreign or domestic, and the organizational development from the craft shop and factory to such concerns as U.S. Steel illustrate the same process of industrial mutation...that incessantly revolutionizes the economic structure from within, incessantly destroying the old one, incessantly creating a new one. This process of Creative Destruction is the essential fact about capitalism. It is what capitalism consists in and what every capitalist concern has got to live in. Capitalism requires the perennial gale of Creative Destruction."

- Joseph A. Schumpeter

I cannot improve upon this. It is descriptive of the system that is free enterprise, but it also identifies one of the major ingredients of success embedded in free enterprise. That "essential fact" is cause for celebration in any objective macro sense, and every one of us lives under the privilege and comfort this creative destruction has produced for centuries.

INCEN-
TIVES

"The mounting burden of taxation not only undermines individual incentives to increased work and earnings, but in a score of ways discourages capital accumulation and distorts, unbalances, and shrinks production. Total real wealth and income is made smaller than it would otherwise be. On net balance there is more poverty rather than less."

- Henry Hazlitt

I want to focus on one of the particular things that Hazlitt says here—that taxation undermines incentives for capital accumulation. He says more here, and much of it is tautologically true (that wealth and income are made smaller by taxation), and on a later page I address the broad impact to incentives that redistributionism represents. But here, I want to focus on incentives for capital accumulation. For the social engineer, this may seem not at all a negative. If the accumulation of wealth by some is a problem, in so much as it merely skews the size of pie slices within the total pie, then perhaps this disincentive is no problem. Indeed, for the social engineer and social justice warrior of today, a capital decumulation amongst the wealthy may seem a noble aim. But alas, there is a problem (you know that was coming).... It is rooted in the zero-sum fallacy—the notion that there is a fixed amount of wealth in the universe and the accumulation of it by one means less available for another. But not only is this not true—the overall pie can and will grow through the productive behavior of human beings meeting the needs of each other—but in stunting the actual *capital formation* that comes from one's capital accumulation, we disincentivize the very savings and investment *that would otherwise benefit others*. Taxes that punish capital leave less capital in the system and disincentivize capital investment. One person's savings is another's borrowings. One person's investments are the source of another's equity, debt, capital projects, hiring, innovation, R&D, etc. In this sense, those who would disincentivize the accumulation of capital for X do far more damage to everyone else than they do to X. Presumably, X already has wealth; but what they have done is cut off the ability of X to use his wealth to create wealth for Y and Z. This is counter-productive, and worse, it is immoral.

"Most of Marx's predictions have failed to materialize, and his labor theory of value and other ideas have been proven wrong. Marx failed to recognize the incentive system built into the capitalist model—consumer choice and the profit motive of the entrepreneur. The irony is that capitalism, not socialism or Marxism, that has liberated the worker from the chains of poverty, monopoly, war, and oppression, and has better achieved Marx's vision of a millennium of hope, peace, abundance, leisure, and aesthetic expression for the 'full' human being."

- Dr. Mark Skousen

The Marxian idea that value is determined by the labor necessary to create it is wrong for a number of reasons. For the advocate of free enterprise, it is the incentives of the system that most rationalize productive human action. If we truly champion liberation from oppression, our economic aims must be the cultivation of liberty and facilitation of incentives that drive such liberation.

"The way to maximize production is to maximize the incentives to production. And the way to do that, as the modern world has discovered, is through the system known as capitalism—the system of private property, free markets, and free enterprise."

- Henry Hazlitt

The most successful of economic ideas are ones that understand incentives, play into incentives, reject disincentives, and seek systems that broadly incentivize what we want in our socio-economic order. Hazlitt understood this, as well as any economist in the last two hundred years. Once you can say the most basic of economic truisms—"we want more production"—you can easily consider what produces the incentive for production. That incentive is the profit motive, embedded in the free enterprise system.

"It is the trend [of debt to GDP] more than anything else that is disturbing. I mean, the trend is more each year, and as you take more each year, it means you are taking a larger and larger share of the new money in the economy. At some point that becomes a disincentive to production or a disincentive in the private sector, and the general economy starts to slow down. I think that the rationale for looking at expenses rather than at the deficit is that the expenses are the amount of money that the government is taking out of the private sector. Whether it takes those by taxes or by borrowing them is kind of a secondary matter. The primary matter is how much money is it taking. That's measured by expenditures."

- Robert L. Bartley

The discovery I had some time back that the size of government relative to the economy was the most important indicator in the economy had a profound impact on me. It explained why the economy has still grown handsomely even in periods of high deficits, where the percentage of the government within the economy was not growing. The key issue was, and is, incentives. A larger government even without deficit spending crowds out the private sector, and ultimately, disincentivizes productive activity. A smaller government with deficit spending is less problematic for economic incentives. It is the belief that incentives matter (human action) that forms my view of government spending relative to the size of the economy.

"There is no more certain way to deter employment than to harass and penalize employers."

- Henry Hazlitt

I am sure we could all think of ways to incentivize hiring if we wanted to. But that conversation will have to wait for another day, since right now the battle must be in proving the folly of all the disincentives we have put up against hiring. From the harassment and general public attitude displayed against employers, to the regulatory environment entrepreneurs must endure, to the utterly pitiful litigious environment that now rules the day, we can forget about incentives for job growth. Our battle must be removing these impediments that exist towards such. We must turn the entire public sentiment and attitude on its head.

"Economists love to talk about incentives, but the bottom line is that people hate being controlled or manipulated, even when done through voluntary institutions. This is one of the most important tensions in capitalism."

- Tyler Cowen

The miracle of markets is that they align incentives with human action. As markets exceed normal exploitation of incentives and transcend into control or manipulation territory, human action inherently resists. In this tension, a valuable service is provided to society—the resistance of control juxtaposed with the benefit of incentives.

"When people who earn more than the average have their 'surplus,' or the greater part of it, seized from them in taxes, and when people who earn less than average have the deficiency, or the greater part of it, turned over to them in hand-outs and doles, the production of all must sharply decline; for the energetic and able who lose their incentive to produce more than the average, and the slothful and unskilled lose their incentive to improve their condition."

- Henry Hazlitt

This binary economic truth—that redistribution cuts at the incentive for the productive to be productive and at the incentive for the non-productive to be productive—is at the heart of a free and virtuous society. We deteriorate freedom when we make the productive less productive, and we deteriorate virtue when we incentivize non-productivity.

"Practically all government attempts to redistribute wealth and income tend to smother productive incentives and lead toward general impoverishment."

- Henry Hazlitt

The economic crime of redistribution is not merely the confiscatory nature of it; it is what happens to incentives in a free society. The redistribution aim in modern economics marginally reduces incentives—but incentives for what? Well, the incentive to work, to invest, to hire, and to create, for starters. So if the aim of economic policy is to discourage work, investment, hiring, and innovation, aggressive redistribution is a good place to start.

"Commerce tends toward rewarding inclusion, broadness, and liberality. Tribal loyalties, ethnic and religious bigotries, and irrational prejudices are bad for business. The merchant class has been conventionally distrusted by tribalist leaders—from the ancient to the modern world—precisely because merchant craft tends to break down barriers between groups."

- Jeffrey Tucker

You can note this as a key tenet in the social organization of a free and virtuous society. You can note it as part of the human flourishing such cooperation in commerce stimulates. But it can never be forgotten—this is intrinsically, an incentive. There are incentives in commerce towards greater trust, inclusion, and cooperation. The rewards he refers to are part of the incentive structure of markets. The beneficiaries are not merely the buyer and seller in a transaction, but the society at-large.

TAX – ATION

"The larger the percentage of the national income taken by taxes the greater the deterrent to private production and employment. When the total tax burden grows beyond a bearable size, the problem of devising taxes that will not discourage and disrupt production becomes insoluble."

- Henry Hazlitt

I would start right here with our understanding of taxes. We most certainly have to find the right revenue mechanism and revenue level to fund the government. And my preference would be for a smaller government, therefore a smaller revenue need. But when we think about the mechanism and the amount, we must always think about these things as in tension with the production needed to foster a healthy economy. Taxes take from economic growth, yet economic growth is where the revenue comes from to pay taxes. Lose sight of this tension point, and you will lose everything.

"While a low capital gains tax is not the only neces-sary ingredient to fostering an entrepreneurial spirit, the lower the rate the more capital will flow from those who have it in surplus to those who are in deficit. It is not the entrepreneur who thinks about the tax he or she will have to pay if the enterprise they undertake is suc-cessful. It is the investor who makes those calculations, which is why at the margin more top-to-bottom capital is created as the rate is lowered."

- Jude Wanniski

Those who favor less taxes on capital implicitly favor more cap-ital formation, and capital formation is the *sine qua non* of an entrepreneurial economy. Inversely, those who favor more tax on capital implicitly favor less capital formation (perhaps explic-itly), and advocate the stifling of the capital the entrepreneur needs to innovate, grow, and prosper. More capital gets from investors to creators when less capital is taxed away. It would be more obvious if it weren't already so completely obvious.

"I would not be averse to eliminating [the capital gain tax] if I thought that were politically feasible. The income was taxed when you first earned it, and then if you invest it should you be taxed again if you invest it successfully? I'm not too concerned about [some who say this will only help the rich]. You can debate who the rich are and who it helps, but I think that my primary interest is that it helps the people who want to get rich; that is, in particular the entrepreneurs which I think are the absolute key to the economy."

- Robert L. Bartley

Is the capital gain tax a double tax on those who pay it? It surely is. But far worse, it is a disincentive to capital formation, needed to fuel the new ideas and new innovations necessary to create new wealth. Capital gain taxes do not hurt those who have already made wealth nearly as much as they hurt those who have not yet done so.

"If you know the position a person takes on taxes, you can tell their whole philosophy. The tax code, once you get to know it, embodies all the essence of life: greed, politics, power, goodness, charity."

- Sheldon S. Cohen

It is sad but true. Does one see coercion as a means of effecting charity? You will see it in their view of taxes. Does one hold to a high view of self-government or a low view that requires an ever-growing state to assume those duties? You will see it in their view of taxes.

"The existence of big government and progressive income taxes guarantees non-neutrality.... With steeply progressive tax rates...inflation [pushes] taxpayers into higher and higher tax brackets even at unchanged real incomes. Taxes [have] to be paid on interest receipts even though the bulk of the high interest rates [represent] inflation premiums. Soaring tax revenues coupled with government's high marginal propensity to spend led to an increasing share of government in the economy."

- Robert A. Mundell

I suppose, in a twisted way, one of the advantages of a steeper progression in tax rates was the audacity it highlighted in how inflation caused higher tax burdens without higher real incomes. At "flatter" (but not flat) tax rates, taxpayers are still exposed to the perversion of what Mundell describes here yet with a subtlety and slowness to it that stems off needed outrage. Inflation and progressive tax rates (the policy prescription of the 1970s) are the worst combination of economic circumstances possible. Sound money and lower marginal rates drive prosperity.

"People don't work to pay taxes; they work and invest for the after-tax return."

- *Dr. Arthur Laffer*

The simple point that Laffer makes here struck at the core of incentives in outlining a tax and economic policy that desperately needed more output after the stagflation of the 1970s: Marginal incentives to work and produce were devastated by high progressive marginal tax rates, and it was influencing behavior—not merely in behavioral decisions that affected capital, but labor as well.

"In fact, I would argue that the level of taxation and of government regulation is a measure of our failure to civilize our society."

- Edward H. Crane

This has always been my argument—that there is a directly inverse relationship between man's self-government and the size of state government. The stronger our self-government, the more noble our virtue, the more robust our families, churches, and communities, the less need we have for a behemoth federal government. The higher the need for behemoth federal government, the more tax and regulation that comes therewith.

"Borrowing imposes a hidden burden upon taxpayers in the short run and an explicit burden in the long run, while taxes impose an explicit short-run burden and a more hidden burden in the long run."

- Richard K. Vedder

Choose your poison. The public seems to be more focused on what they can see and what hurts them short term. But both borrowing and taxes impose burdens in both the short term and the long term. The rest is just noise around how visible and detectable and felt these burdens are.

"We have come to love income tax laws so much that we have chosen to have a lot of them…. The resulting loss of efficiency in our economy, and cost of private sector compliance are staggering."

- Gordon D. Henderson

We couldn't leave it alone with high taxes—we had to create high complexity and high burdens to go along with the high costs! So it always is, any diminishment of freedom results in multiple ways to lose. The greed and recklessness and power aspiration of government is evidenced in the tax code, yet all at once so is the inefficiency, bureaucracy, and general incompetence. A truly losing combination of circumstances!

"All taxation, however disguised, is a loss per se...it is the duty, and the sacred duty, of Government to take only from the people what is necessary to the proper discharge of the public service; and that taxation in any other mode is simply in one shape or another, legalized robbery."

- Richard Cartwright

Treating the tax code as a pure funding mechanism for government is right and proper, and of course, invites public discussion on what kind of government is wanted, and therefore to be paid for. But to treat the tax code as a means of administering social policy, of punishing one group or rewarding another, is unethical. Using the tax code as a redistributionist ponzi distorts its proper function and usurps freedom and property.

"Supply-side economics began as a policy system alternative to Keynesian demand-side models. It was based on a policy mix that delivered price stability through monetary discipline, and economic stimulation of employment and growth through the tax and regulatory systems. It concluded that cuts in marginal tax rates were needed to create output incentives to spur the economy, and tight money would produce price stability. The economy embarked on one of its longest-ever expansions at the same time that inflation was increasingly brought under control. The new policies shifted the Phillips curve downward and to the left, allowing unemployment and inflation to decrease at the same time."

- Robert A. Mundell

The policy mix the great Mundell refers to came out of the early 1980s and helped promote one of the great periods of prosperity in world history. The Volcker-led Fed embarked upon the politically unpopular decision to raise rates until monetary excess was extracted from the system, *at the same time* that output exploded as supply-side tax cuts produced substantial incentives for productivity. Much of economic theory is, well, theory, and is rooted in analysis and logical adjudication. The statements here are more empirical. The Phillips Curve theory that growth and inflation were positively correlated was turned on its head, as growth came out of marginal tax cuts, and price stability came out of counter-inflationary.

CREDIT & SOUND MONEY

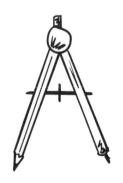

"What is fundamental to economic theory is that there is no constant relation between changes in the quantity of money and in prices. Changes in the supply of money affect individual prices and wages in different ways. The metaphor of the term price level is misleading."

- Ludwig Von Mises

There is no such thing as an aggregate price level, and if there were, by the time you calculated such it would have changed a nano-second later, with no quantitative way to determine why. Variable relationships exist in the economy that defy reason to try and measure or handicap. Why is this important? Because some of the great monetary monstrosities of all time have been committed trying to manage or control something (the price level) that doesn't even exist, let alone subject itself to management or control.

"Prices do not move all in sync in response to changes in money supply. Prices respond to the forces of supply and demand for that particular product or service, and prices are also impacted by changes in the demand for and supply of money. Separating these forces by looking at prices is necessarily qualitative, conjectural and complex."

- Christopher Mayer

It can thus be said that attempts to create an economic outcome by trying to manipulate the money supply is futile. Prices are dynamic, not at all monolithic, and are "messed with" at our own peril. Messing with the soundness of money provides far more risk than reward and always has.

"In practice [monetary management] is merely a high-sounding euphemism for continuous currency debasement. It consists of constant lying in order to support constant swindling.... They hold paper promises whose value falls with every bureaucratic whim. And they are suavely assured that only hopelessly antiquated minds dream of returning to truth and honesty and solvency..."

- Henry Hazlitt

Whether one believes the worst about the intentions of "monetary managers" or not, there is no doubt that the promises of monetary management as a means of increasing sound money have proven hollow, and that instead, monetary management has become politicized and may now very well have evolved into one of the greatest (and riskiest) economic experiments in history.

"Money is not an invention of the state. It is not the product of a legislative act. Even the sanction of political authority is not necessary for its existence. Certain commodities came to be money quite naturally, as the result of economic relationships that were independent of the power of the state."

- Carl Menger

If one accepts money to be a medium of exchange, then one has to believe there was money before there was a state that regulated it. Mediums for exchange exist outside of state inventions and legislative declarations, even though our Constitution gives certain regulatory authority to the state around such. The relevance here is that the soundness of money is determined by its sanctity as a medium of exchange. Wild price fluctuations undermine that soundness, and wild price fluctuations in the medium of exchange are almost always state-created.

"There is a strange idea aboard, held by all monetary cranks, that credit is something a banker gives to a man. Credit, on the contrary, is something a man already has. He has it, perhaps, because he already has marketable assets of a greater cash value than the loan for which he is asking. Or he has it because his character and past record have earned it. He brings it into the bank with him. That is why the banker makes him the loan."

- Henry Hazlitt

Credit is an asset on one side of the accounting ledger and a liability on the other side. And to the side that extends the credit, it holds the asset. That asset is secured by something—or it would not be considered an asset. Whether it be the financial credit-worthiness of the borrower, the track record of performance and capacity that helped underwrite the loan, or just the public reputation—credit is the instrument by which money supply really grows in our economy (contrary to popular opinion). Therefore, the real risk to sound money is bad credit. And therefore, the character of who receives credit (who holds the liability) is the make-or-break point of sound money.

"The 1970s started off as a disaster, from the standpoint of economic stability, but nevertheless, it set in motion a learning mechanism that would not have taken place in its absence. The lesson was that inflation, budget deficits, big debts and big government are all detrimental to public well-being and that the cost of correcting them is so high that no democratic government wants to repeat the experience."

- Robert A. Mundell

There is no question, politically, that the 1970s made politicians care about the impact of inflation and taxes, as voters learned to despise what both did to their quality of life. The problem is that big government becomes entrenched, and it is the correction of bad policy that Mundell speaks of that governments now seek to avoid and not the bad policy itself. Elected officials are incentivized to promote a "free lunch"—that bad policy can be cured without pain. It cannot be.

> *"All loans, in the eyes of honest borrowers, must eventually be repaid. All credit is debt. Proposals for an increased volume of credit, therefore, are merely another name for proposals for an increased burden of debt. They would seem considerably less inviting if they were habitually referred to by the second name instead of by the first."*
>
> *- Henry Hazlitt*

There is such a thing as productive debt, and it is, by definition, limited to those times the debt is used to fund productivity. It still carries a cost, but for a business targeting a 20 percent return on a capital investment, a 5 percent cost of debt to build it may seem quite worthwhile. Even then, the total ratios and stress-testing of what could go wrong must be measured and understood.

Our society's relationship to debt is not measured by productive vs. unproductive debt. The government uses it to fund a system of transfer payments (no wealth is created), and individuals use it to fund consumption (wealth is actually destroyed). Calling a spade a spade would change the outlook for many.

"It is Orwellian to refer to newly printed government money as 'savings.' Whatever the merits or demerits of 'printing press' money, it is not the same as savings. The word savings describes money that has been earned, and having been earned, is not spent but rather set aside for emergency or investment use.... The government's new money will eventually destroy traditional savings [and]...will ultimately erode the purchasing power of traditional savings and thus ruin the saver, especially the small saver."

- Hunter Lewis

Such bastardization of the English language as to refer to government borrowings, printings, or expenditures as "savings" is, indeed, Orwellian (it facilitates greater government intrusion), but it is also economically indefensible. Savings are always and forever money earned then set aside as reserves or investment. Government expenditures are always and forever money taken from the private sector (out of national savings).

"It is possible to increase paper-money income to any amount by debasing the currency. But real income can only be increased by working harder or more efficiently, saving more, investing more, and producing more."

- Henry Hazlitt

There's no free lunch. All attempts to increase income without increasing work, efficiency, saving, investment, and productivity are futile. Worse, they are fraud. They are manipulations and acts of theft. Increasing the standard of living comes from human action—from the sum total of wealth which is embedded in productivity and investment. The rest is basically the stuff that put the Enron folks in jail.

"[Inflation] is a way to take people's wealth from them without having to openly raise taxes. Inflation is the most universal tax of all."

- Thomas Sowell

This is a truism with many centuries of precedent. And while it is, indeed, universal, it also is highly regressive, which is one of the reasons it is so unforgivable that those who most loudly defend a progressive income tax system advocate policies that create the regressive result of inflation. Inflationary effects in consumer goods hurts lower income people more, because the price of those goods represents a higher percentage of their income than those in higher income tiers. This is mathematically undeniable, yet also easily ignored by those who advocate for such policies. Inflation is like that—easy to ignore its impact year by year, but impossible decade by decade.

"If time is money, then interest rates are the price of time."
- John Mauldin

What a simple but eloquent way to understand what interest rates are and why they exist. Our money has a purpose, now. To part with our money (either because of lending it out for someone else's use or investing in the equity reward of a business or project) means a delay in that purpose. The "interest rate" is the price we set on the time we will be parted from our money.

"My fundamental disagreement...with all Keynesian and Monetarist demand-siders, is that you devalue the importance of money's function as a unit of account. In classical economics—which concentrates entirely on production (supply), not consumption (demand)— transactors in the exchange economy have more concern with money as a constant accounting unit than as a medium of exchange or store of value. In producing and exchanging across time and space, Keynesians and Monetarists automatically downgrade this function of money as they attempt to manipulate the national aggregate economy.... Keynesians cannot break the habit of trying to change the terms of trade with other countries by manipulating the value of the accounting unit.... What a mess they created."

- Jude Wanniski

As I have gotten older and had to fight harder to control my weight, I have often used a similar analogy to what Wanniski uses here, that I cannot manage my weight by adjusting my scale. What we want as free marketeers is, indeed, money to be a mere unit of account. Sound money leads to a stable medium of exchange, where market forces can adjudicate the value of the goods and services transacting, but the accounting unit is reliable.

"The goal, then, should not be to manage prices. The goal should be to ensure that prices are free to fluctuate. Therefore, an emphasis should be placed not on containing prices, but on eliminating obstacles that attempt to change prices to something other than what is supported in the marketplace."

- Christopher Mayer

Policymakers get this wrong constantly, but I am not at all convinced they get it wrong by accident. Ideally, stable prices should be the aim of public policy, with fluctuations coming from those things impacted by human action—effort, demand, tastes, risks, etc. Marketplace forces may change prices, but the centralized planning or manipulation of prices is both distortive and destructive to the very efforts we want from economic actors—namely, risk-taking, effort, and productive behavior.

"One product is always ultimately bought with another, even when paid for in the first instance with money."

- Jean-Baptiste Say

The profundity in this truism cannot be overstated. If you accept money as a medium of exchange, the delay between one product's payment for another's is no matter at all. Ultimately, "money" brings divisibility and time optionality to barter exchange, and with that, significant complexity. But none of that changes the truth of what Say here says. We are always exchanging goods and services with one another. Money simply allows us to do such with incredible customization and convenience.

"If a government resorts to inflation, that is, creates money in order to cover its budget deficits or expands credit in order to stimulate business, then no power on earth, no gimmick, device, trick or even indexation can prevent its economic consequences."

- Henry Hazlitt

There is no free lunch, indeed. The idea that any government can make money *ex nihilo* is just as much wishful thinking as the idea that a government can spend money without restraint, without consequence. Pick your poison, but whether it be price inflation, misallocation of resources, the bursting of an asset bubble, or generational suppression of growth—or perhaps some combination of multiple items on this list—they are unavoidable.

"Your argument is that technological advance should result in a general price decline. But to a classical economist, that's like saying that as modern golfers hit the ball further and further with better equipment, the yardstick should gradually lengthen. When the dollar is kept [stable], technological advances are translated into shorter units of time needed to produce goods and services."

- Jude Wanniski

Prices may come down in a market economy from competitive forces at play, but the advances that we want in a growing economy are not price declines (or increases), as much as improved quality of life in the process of producing goods and services. The focus on price makes the unit of measurement the activity instead of the underlying activity. It is highly convoluted. While ample disagreements exist as to how to achieve sound and stable money, it is the disregard for the objective of sound money that has been most disruptive.

"The most obvious and yet the oldest and most stubborn error on which the appeal of inflation rests is that of confusing 'money' with 'wealth'.... Real wealth, of course, consists in what is produced and consumed: the food we eat, the clothes we wear, the houses we live in. It is railways and roads and motor cars; ships and planes and factories; schools and churches and theaters; pianos, paintings and books. Yet so powerful is the verbal ambiguity that confuses money with wealth, that even those who at times recognize the confusion will slide back into it in the course of their reasoning."

- Henry Hazlitt

Money is a medium of exchange. It can be stable or not. When it is not, it is nearly always the fault of a policy or policymaker. Wealth is the by-product of what we produce. We can't artificially create wealth, only money. The inability to understand this is the cause of unspeakable economic error.

POLIT-
ICAL
POWER

"Viewed as a means to the end of political freedom, economic arrangements are important because of their effect on the concentration or dispersion of power. The kind of economic organization that provides economic freedom directly, namely, competitive capitalism, also promotes political freedom because it separates economic power from political power and in this way enables the one to offset the other."

- Milton Friedman

This masterful quote is almost self-explanatory, but the message behind it is profoundly important. A vicious cycle exists where there is limited political freedom that facilitates limited economic freedom (let alone civic freedom). But a virtuous cycle exists where economic power is separated (as much as possible) from political power. Limiting the size of government (political power) is the only way to limit the capacity for using political power to enhance economic power.

"Our freedom of choice in a competitive society rests on the fact that, if one person refuses to satisfy our wishes, we can turn to another. But if we face a monopolist we are at his absolute mercy. And an authority directing the whole economic system of the country would be the most powerful monopolist conceivable...it would have complete power to decide what we are to be given and on what terms. It would not only decide what commodities and services were to be available and in what quantities; it would be able to direct their distributions between persons to any degree it liked."

- F.A. Hayek

Excessive political power can never remain a purely political problem. It can never remain a civic problem. It must always become an economic problem. Absolute political power undermines the *sine qua non* of economic freedom—competitive choice. The control available to political absolutists defies our imagination's ability to comprehend.

"History suggests only that capitalism is a necessary condition for political freedom. Clearly it is not a sufficient condition. Fascist Italy and Fascist Spain, Germany at various times in the last seventy years, Japan before World Wars I and II, tzarist Russia in the decades before World War I—are all societies that cannot conceivably be described as politically free. Yet, in each, private enterprise was the dominant form of economic organization. It is therefore clearly possible to have economic arrangements that are fundamentally capitalist and political arrangements that are not free."

- Milton Friedman

China would be the other example under and after Deng Xiaoping. "Necessary but not sufficient." A truly free society will have economic, political, and civic freedom, and all three will feed on each other. Having one enhances the possibilities with the others, but it guarantees no such thing. One can have marginal economic freedom without full political freedom, but one cannot have political freedom without economic freedom. One (economic) makes the other (political) possible but not assured. And the lack of one (economic) makes the other (political) impossible. The durability of an imperfect economic freedom in a politically unfree society remains a sizable question on the world stage.

"A society that puts equality before freedom will get neither. A society that puts freedom before equality will get a high degree of both.... Underlying most arguments against the free market is a lack of belief in freedom itself."

- Milton Friedman

This chicken-or-egg discussion is addressed perfectly by Milton Friedman. Subordinating freedom to equality means, by definition, the attempt of a disinterested third party (government) to effect a social result by some form of coercion. Equality, or any other social result, can only come about sustainably from an environment of freedom. Coercion cannot create equality—only the appearance of a temporary equality. If one truly believes in freedom, they must believe in freedom as the precursor to other social aims.

SOCIAL ORGANI- ZATION

"The basic problem of social organization is how to coordinate the economic activities of large numbers of people. Even in relatively backward societies, extensive division of labor and specialization of function are required to make effective use of available resources. In advanced societies, the scale on which coordination is needed, to take full advantage of the opportunities offered by modern science and technology, is enormously greater. Literally millions of people are involved in providing one another with their daily bread, let alone with their yearly automobiles. The challenge to the believer in liberty is to reconcile this widespread interdependence with individual freedom."

- Milton Friedman

The [individual] human action embedded in this miracle of social cooperation is both caused by a free and virtuous society, and the free and virtuous society is enhanced by this social cooperation. The individual and collective benefits of this social contract are a sight to behold; interventions from disinterested third parties are its greatest threat.

"The man of system...is apt to be very wise in his own conceit; and is often so enamored with the supposed beauty of his own ideal plan of government, that he cannot suffer the smallest deviation from any part of it. He goes on to establish it completely and in all its parts, without any regard either to the great interests, or to the strong prejudices which may oppose it. He seems to imagine that he can arrange the different members of a great society with as much ease as the hand arranges the different pieces upon a chess board. He does not consider that the pieces upon the chess board have no other principle of motion besides that which the hand impresses upon them; but that, in the great chess board of human society, every single piece has a principle of motion of its own, altogether different from that which the legislature might choose to impress upon it. If those two principles coincide and act in the same direction, the game of human society will go on easily and harmoniously and is very likely to be happy and successful. If they are opposite or different, the game will go on miserably, and the society must be at all times in the highest degree of disorder."

- Adam Smith

There is nothing—nothing—I could say to improve on this mastery.

"For all the quantifiable variables available to modern economics, capitalism is not a technical or scientific system; it is basically a system for diffusing authority and decision-making power, and letting people have what they want. It argues that since market success is a matter of speaking to people's preferences, leaving decisions at the level of the individual exchange is almost always going to work better—to produce more wealth and more happiness. That doesn't mean society has to live at the mercy of base and degraded preferences, but it means we get beyond them by educating people's preferences and judgments, rather than by taking them over—by moral education, not by rational control."

- Yuval Levin

We do not doubt the need for a civilized society to be socially organized by some framework. The question is which framework will create the best outcome—a centralized command-control one, or one in which free people individually transact, each in pursuit of a better life. This question does answer itself to some degree, but we err to ignore the final portion of Levin's exhortation: wise and moral discernment sits at the foundation of optimal social organization in a market economy.

"The argument for liberty is not an argument against organization, which is one of the most powerful tools human reason can employ, but an argument against all exclusive, privileged, monopolistic organization, against the use of coercion to prevent others from doing better."

- *F.A. Hayek*

The straw man argument most often used against those of us who oppose top-down command-control management of society is that we favor chaos and disorder. Quite the contrary! History has taught us, validated by all we know about human nature, that the results of statist social organization is chaotic tyranny at worst and coercive cronyism at best. On the contrary, the fruits of social organization rooted in reason and voluntary cooperation have been unprecedented peace and prosperity.

"The vices of modernism come from the master vice of Pride, the vice so characteristic of an actual or wannabe aristocracy. It is prideful overreaching to think that social engineering can work, that a smart lad at a blackboard can outwit the wisdom of the world or the ages, that a piece of machinery like statistical significance can tell you how big or small a number is."

- Deirdre N. McCloskey

There is a huge reference to "the knowledge problem" here—and with that, the problem of top-down social organization. It is not merely the inefficiency or inadequate price discovery that renders such social engineering foolish. At its core, this very aspiration is prideful. It reflects a disdain for human experience and imputes to an elite few a mastery of the masses that no one deserves and no one can dare handle.

"The theories of the social sciences do not consist of 'laws' in the sense of empirical rules about the behavior of objects definable in physical terms. All that the theory of the social sciences attempts is to provide a technique of reasoning which assists us in connecting individual facts, but which, like logic or mathematics, is not about the facts. It can, therefore, and this is the second point, never be verified or falsified by reference to facts."

- F.A. Hayek

This lack of ability to verify or falsify the theories of today's social scientists is the most frightening component of organized social management. Failures do not worry those who believe they can masterfully control the affairs of society, because the lack of specificity and factual foundation gives them a never-ending wiggle room to adjust, to modify, to move on, all without accountability for the failure of their broken theories. They want all the benefits of practicing a "science" (authority, credibility, presumption of expertise) but none of the accountability. It's a pretty good deal for them, and a lousy one for the rest of us.

"It has never been the argument of most of those who favor markets that economic freedom and free exchange are somehow sufficient to reduce poverty. These things are certainly indispensable (witness the failure of planned economies to solve the problem of scarcity), but they're not enough. Among other things, stable governments that provide infrastructure, property arrangements that identify clearly who owns what, and, above all, the rule of law are just as essential.... The lack of rule of law not only ranks among the biggest obstacles to their ability [of developing nations] to generate wealth on a sustainable basis, but also hampers their capacity to address economic issues in a just manner.... Market-oriented scholars have been underscoring for several decades the vital importance of values and institutions in explaining the causes of economic growth and decline."

- Dr. Samuel Gregg

The great straw man advocates of a free and virtuous society must avoid walking into is the accusation that we believe society can be organized optimally by pure *laissez-faire* with no regard for the peripheral components necessary to optimize freedom and flourishing. While the socialist embraces top-down social organization, and the radical individualist may advocate a stateless social cooperative, our vision for society must be rooted in the rule of law, defense of property rights, and equally important, the values and virtues that will either see market economies flourish or else languish.

"The most manifest characteristic of human beings is their diversity. The freer an economy is, the more this human diversity of knowledge will be manifested. By contrast, political power originates in top-down processes—governments, monopolies, regulators, and elite institutions—all attempting to quell human diversity and impose order. Thus, power always seeks centralization."

- George Gilder

Human beings have diverse experiences, perspectives, talents, and priorities. Modernity claims to celebrate diversity, and yet what most unleashes the glory of human diversity is freedom. Social organization from the top squashes this diversity, and worse, no one seems to appreciate the irony.

"From the fact that people are very different it follows that, if we treat them equally, the result must be inequality in their actual position, and that the only way to place them in an equal position would be to treat them differently. Equality before the law and material equality are therefore not only different but are in conflict with each other; and we can achieve either one or the other, but not both at the same time."

- F.A. Hayek

The damage done in the pursuit of equality surpasses the damage done by inequality exponentially. It is not our inability to achieve equal outcomes that is shameful; it is the defiance of logic and reality that such a pursuit represents. The idea that we would seek to organize a society around such a notion is dangerous, futile, and ultimately, fatal.

"Fundamentally, there are only two ways of coordinating the economic activities of millions. One is central direction involving the use of coercion—the technique of the army and of the modern totalitarian state. The other is voluntary cooperation of individuals—the technique of the marketplace. The possibility of coordination through voluntary cooperation rests on the elementary—yet frequently denied—proposition that both parties to an economic transaction benefit from it, provided the transaction is bi-laterally voluntary and informed. Exchange can therefore bring about coordination without coercion. A working model of a society organized through voluntary exchange is a true private enterprise exchange economy that we have been calling competitive capitalism."

- Milton Friedman

Out of free exchange comes a social cooperation that prospers both parties. Out of coercion comes totalitarianism, which is to say, tyranny.

"Government-to-government foreign aid promotes stat-ism, centralized planning, socialism, dependence, pau-perization, inefficiency, and waste. It prolongs the pov-erty it is designed to cure. Voluntary private investment in private enterprise, on the other hand, promotes cap-italism, production, independence, and self-reliance."

- Henry Hazlitt

Few subjects have generated more discussion and experimenta-tion over the last thirty years than that of foreign aid. And few subjects have resulted in more lessons learned the hard way than foreign aid. From all-out corruption to enabling bad actors to the tragedy of a cycle of dependency, divorcing foreign aid from the engine of wealth creation, from the time-tested tools of produc-tion and entrepreneurship, has been an abject disaster.

"What sense would it make to classify a man as hand-icapped because he is in a wheelchair today, if he is expected to be walking again in a month, and competing in track meets before the year is out? Yet Americans are given 'class' labels on the basis of their transient location in the income stream. If most Americans do not stay in the same broad income bracket for even a decade, their repeatedly changing 'class' makes class itself a nebulous concept. Yet the intelligentsia are habituated, if not addicted, to seeing the world in class terms, just as they constantly speak of the deliberate actions of a personified 'society' when trying to explain the results of systemic interactions among millions of individuals."

- Thomas Sowell

The language of class is second only in offensiveness to the mentality behind it. It is used as a device by self-interested ideologues who require a construct of oppression. In fact, unlike race and gender, one's "class" can (and very often does) change in a society that celebrates vertical mobility. For the aspirational society, "class" should be a very temporary description. The obsession over class speaks not to the limitations of such aspiration, but the agenda of those who would hold people back.

"Well first of all, tell me: Is there some society you know that doesn't run on greed? You think Russia doesn't run on greed? You think China doesn't run on greed? What is greed? Of course, none of us are greedy, it's only the other fellow who's greedy. The world runs on individuals pursuing their separate interests. The great achievements of civilization have not come from government bureaus. Einstein didn't construct his theory under order from a bureaucrat. Henry Ford didn't revolutionize the automobile industry that way. In the only cases in which the masses have escaped from the kind of grinding poverty you're talking about, the only cases in recorded history, are where they have had capitalism and largely free trade. If you want to know where the masses are worse off, worst off, it's exactly in the kinds of societies that depart from that. So that the record of history is absolutely crystal clear, that there is no alternative way so far discovered of improving the lot of the ordinary people that can hold a candle to the productive activities that are unleashed by the free-enterprise system.

Is political self-interest really nobler than economic self-interest? Where in the world do you find these angels who are going to organize society for us?"

- Milton Friedman

Some of you may recognize this from a famous appearance on the Phil Donahue show in 1979. I would be happy to have its sentiment serve as the fundamental takeaway of the entire book. It addresses the disingenuous claim that the market actor is greedy and points to the greed of the collectivist. It reaffirms the historical case for a market economy lifting the masses out of poverty. It speaks to productive activities—the essence of free enterprise—as unleashing that which brings about human flourishing. And fundamentally, it is the case for social organization, not out of command and control, but rather free and cooperative pursuits.

PRI-
VATE
PROP-
ERTY

"If history could teach us anything, it would be that private property is inextricably linked with civilization."

- Ludwig Von Mises

One of the great achievements of the collectivist has been to frame discussions of private property around an implied greed of the holder. Putting a negative connotation around private property puts her defenders on the defensive, when in fact, the existence of private property, and a system that defends and enables and cultivates private property, is demonstrably necessary for a functioning civilization. History leaves us no doubt—where there is no private property, or legal system to defend such, chaos reigns. Where there is a healthy respect for the God-given concept of private property and private ownership, a flourishing civilization becomes possible.

"Those who founded the United States of America, and wrote the Constitution, saw property rights as essential for safeguarding all other rights. The right to free speech, for example, would be meaningless if criticisms of the authorities could lead to whatever you owned being seized in retaliation."

- Thomas Sowell

Private property are not words found in the Bill of Rights. Rather, they are the *sine qua non* of all the other rights enumerated therein.

"Life, faculties, production—in other words, individuality, liberty, property—this is man. And in spite of the cunning of artful political leaders, these three gifts from God precede all human legislation, and are superior to it. Life, liberty, and property do not exist because men have made laws. On the contrary, it was the fact that life, liberty, and property existed beforehand that caused men to make laws in the first place."

- Frédéric Bastiat

This "chicken or egg" issue is crucial if we are to defend the rights that sit at the foundation of a free society. Once we say that we own private property because we have laws that grant us such, we have made private ownership subservient to the state. The state is the actor that should defend private property rights, but it is not, and cannot be, the actor that grants property rights. A flourishing society must get both of these things right: (1) Property and rights are inseparable, and (2) the state must serve as the impartial defender of such.

"I think that nothing is so important for freedom as recognizing in the law each individual's natural right to property, and giving individuals a sense that they own something that they're responsible for, that they have control over, and that they can dispose of."

- Milton Friedman

The conditions for private ownership are laid out here—responsibility, control, and right of disposition. Private ownership and the protection of such is as old as the eighth commandment, but so are the benefits that flow from private property—greater stewardship, cultivation of individual responsibility, and wiser allocation of resources.

"Private property is a natural fruit of labor, a product of intense activity of man, acquired through his energetic determination to ensure and develop with his own strength his own existence and that of his family, and to create for himself and his own an existence of just freedom, not only economic, but also political, cultural and religious."

- Pope Pius XII

This mid-20th century Pope understood what John Paul II would understand so well just twenty-five years later—that contra the Marxism of the 20th century, private property facilitated the human things. Rather than being corrosive to the soul, the human activity that stewarding private property created was good for the whole being of man in multiple facets of life.

"A people averse to the institution of private property is without the first elements of freedom."

- Lord Acton

The *sine qua non* of freedom is private property. A human who cannot freely own, steward, and make decisions around that which he owns will not be able to maintain his for speech, assembly, or worship, either. A low regard for private property inevitably means no regard for freedom; and where there is high regard for freedom, there will be high regard for private property.

"The system of private property is the most important guaranty of freedom, not only for those who own property, but scarcely less for those who do not."

- F.A. Hayek

A society that defends private property is a society of law and order, of self-preservation, of shared incentives. Protection of private property not only provides bare essential rights and liberties to the owners of private property, but to those aspiring to own property as well. We do not need to think merely of land, real estate, or real assets here. Sovereignty over one's bank accounts, stock portfolio, intellectual property patents, cars, toys, and clothes are all at the heart of a functioning society.

INDIVID-UAL RESPON-SIBILITY

"Freedom to order our own conduct in the sphere where material circumstances force a choice upon us, and responsibility for the arrangement of our own life according to our own conscience, is the air in which alone moral sense grows and in which moral values are daily recreated in the free decision of the individual. Responsibility, not to a superior, but to one's own conscience, the awareness of a duty not exacted by compulsion, the necessity to decide which of the things one values are to be sacrificed to others, and to bear the consequences of one's own decision, are the very essence of any morals which deserve the name."

- *F.A. Hayek*

Indeed, there can be no moral formation when individual responsibility is equated to compulsion. When individuals are left free not just to do the right thing, but to suffer the consequences for doing the wrong thing, we have not only built a terrain for economic justice and opportunity, but the landscape from which morality can exist.

"Allowing people the freedom to pursue their own interests (within the limits of just conduct) is the best and only sustainable way to achieve societal progress. For individuals to develop and have a chance at happiness, they must be free to make their own choices and mistakes, rather than be forced to accept choices made for them by others."

- Charles G. Koch

"Earned success" is empirically proven to be one of the primary sources of happiness and lasting satisfaction in our lives. Along with meaningful relationships, the *telos* of our pursuits of success and productive achievement serve as the foundation for a life well-lived. Earning this success requires freedom, and it requires the freedom to fail. Out of the freedom to fail comes the opportunity to transcend failure. And I can think of nothing that brings more dignity and lasting joy to the human person in God's created order than transcending failure.

"Some paradox of our nature leads us, when once we have made our fellow men the objects of our enlightened interest, to go on to make them objects of our pity, then of our wisdom, ultimately of our coercion."

- Lionel Trilling

Any view of social order that does not start with individual responsibility leads to coercion. To deny one the consequences of their decisions, even if well-intentioned, is to make them an object of pity, and ultimately to impose upon them our wishes for their life. Coercion is the implied end result, whereas rooting our views in an expectation of individual responsibility allows for agency, it allows for participation in either the good or bad results of what they choose, and it avoids a world where we must ultimately coerce people to act as we wish, because we have never allowed them to end up in the right place all on their own.

"Liberty not only means that the individual has both the opportunity and the burden of choice; it also means that he must bear the consequences of his actions and will receive praise or blame for them. Liberty and responsibility are inseparable."

- F.A. Hayek

How much more self-explanatory can this be? This symmetrical relationship between liberty and responsibility is not something to be feared, resisted, or viewed as "50 percent good news." It is in the nature of things, and indeed, the two rely on each other. Take away one, and the other will die.

"Family is a codeword for constraint; families and family values place constraints on individuals more effectively than any other institution, including government. [The Christian ethic] seeks a society in which all are constrained; they reject big government for failing at constraint, and for undermining those institutions, like the family, that have a chance at succeeding."

- Tyler Cowen

Big government is as big as self-government is lacking. This axiomatic truth is at the heart of the relationship between the citizen and the state. Mediating institutions, the family having the most leverage of them all, serve as the effective administrators of self-government, sacrifice, cooperation, and constraint. The incentives are aligned. Civilization is a testimony to the relative success of the institution of family in generating constraint and the failure of the state in doing so.

"The reduced sense of responsibility and the absence of effective volition in turn explain the ordinary citizen's ignorance and lack of judgment in matters of domestic and foreign policy which are if anything more shocking in the case of educated people and of people who are successfully active in non-political walks of life than it is with uneducated people in humble stations."

- Joseph A. Schumpeter

A decline of individual responsibility leads to an environment of repeatedly unsuccessful and unproductive public policy, and unwise public policy leads to a decline of individual responsibility. This negative feedback loop is as dangerous as anything in public life, if for no other reason, then how it successfully obfuscates the cause and effect, making resolution almost impossible.

"Everyone carries a part of society on his shoulders; no one is relieved of his share of responsibility by others. And no one can find a safe way out for himself if society is sweeping toward destruction. Therefore, everyone, in his own interests, must thrust himself vigorously into the intellectual battle. None can stand aside with unconcern; the interest of everyone hangs on the result. Whether he chooses or not, every man is drawn into the great historical struggle, the decisive battle into which our epoch has plunged us."

- Ludwig Von Mises

Two categories of concern are highlighted here: The intellectual nature of the battle, and the moral consequences of disengagement. Apathy is not an option.

"We seem to be getting closer and closer to a situation where nobody is responsible for what they did but we are all responsible for what somebody else did."

- Thomas Sowell

This is not just a clever or cute way of identifying something so culturally frustrating to many of us. It is an inevitability in any society that allows individual responsibility to break down. The more we advocate freeing people of the responsibility of their decisions, the more we advocate transferring the responsibility of their decisions to someone else. What is not an option is that no one has to hold the bag. The piper will be paid, and all we are haggling over is whether or not the individual actor should pay or the rest of us.

*"The ethic of conviction and the ethic of responsibility are
not opposites. They are complementary to one another."*

- Max Weber

A responsible person is faithful to their convictions, and a person of convictions will be more responsible in their personal and public life. The two are not merely complementary but inseparable. Responsibility cannot exist without convictions that guide such responsibility. And convictions that do not lead to responsible decision-making are not convictions at all but fantasies or frauds. The economic ramifications to this are felt in formation. Out of this formation that reflects both conviction and responsible living comes the social dynamic that facilitates trust in a market economy.

"Once the principle is admitted that it is the duty of the government to protect the individual against his own foolishness, no serious objections can be advanced against further encroachments."

- Ludwig Von Mises

We refer to this as the problem of the lack of limiting principle. Opening the door to the government as the defender of the individual against themselves lacks any sort of coherent limiting principle and has been shown to lead to great folly in public policy. Not only does this view of the citizen and the state excessively empower the state, it infantilizes the citizen—the worse sin of the two.

"Real poverty is less a state of income than a state of mind."

- George Gilder

This is in no way to belittle the tragedy of poverty conditions or to deny the temporal misfortunes that may fall upon earnest men and women. But systemically, a state of mind exists that creates a nearly perfect immunity against poverty, and that state of mind is one of individual responsibility. Character, tenacity, resilience, and perseverance represent a state of mind that will stem off poverty more than any government program. That state of mind will create income, but better than that, that state of mind will stave off poverty of spirit.

"A movement whose main promise is the relief from responsibility cannot but be antimoral in its effect, however lofty the ideals to which it owes its birth. Can there be much doubt that the feeling of personal obligation to remedy inequities, where our individual power permits, has been weakened rather than strengthened, that both the willingness to bear responsibility and the consciousness that it is our own individual duty to know how to choose have been perceptibly impaired?.... There is much to suggest that we have in fact become more tolerant toward particular abuses and much more indifferent to inequities in individual cases, since we have fixed our eyes on an entirely different system in which the state will set everything right. It may even be, as has been suggested, that the passion for collective action is a way in which we now without compunction collectively indulge in that selfishness which as individuals we had learned a little to restrain."

- F.A. Hayek

This is a philosophy of ethics that we simply must absorb! A gradual transition of the moral agency of the individual to the state can only lead to the demoralization of the individual. This removal of responsibility from the core of society has not created a collectively more unified and behaved society, but rather one in which restraint and order are outsourced, before they are lost all together.

"To believe in personal responsibility would be to destroy the whole special role of the anointed, whose vision casts them in the role of rescuers of people treated unfairly by 'society.'"

- Thomas Sowell

No matter what we may think of the intentions of some who never fail to provide absolution for those who have neglected individual responsibility, there absolutely exists a conflict of interest. This vision of society creates one class of people whose job it is to rescue, and one class of people whose function is to be rescued by the other class. This vision is not merely to be rejected because of the arrogance and ignorance of the former; it is to be rejected because of how it would rob the latter of their dignity. Advocating for individual responsibility is nothing more than viewing all mankind as being made in the image of God, and possessing value and worth that those who would treat them as objects of pity do not believe they have.

"Citizens who over-rely on their government to do everything not only become dependent on their government, they end up having to do whatever the government demands. In the meantime, their initiative and self-respect are destroyed."

- Charles G. Koch

The vicious cycle here is unspeakable. The human spirit is crushed by dependency, and the role of the individual as a serf to the authoritative wishes of he who rules metastasizes into a truly dysfunctional sort of oppression. A crushed human spirit where dignity is suffocated, all in the name of government "helping" those whose God-given purpose it has stripped.

"Differences in habits and attitudes are differences in human capital, just as much as differences in knowledge and skills—and such differences create differences in economic outcomes."

- Thomas Sowell

Often times, habits and attitudes can make a *bigger* difference in economic outcomes than even knowledge and skills. No attempt to manipulate an equal economic outcome can ever succeed, and the reason is embedded in this reality right here. The differences of human capital always create different outcomes. Human capital is, indeed, the combination of our habits, attitudes, and yes, abilities. Individual responsibility supports the habits and attitudes that drive positive outcomes.

"Outside the sphere of individual responsibility there is neither goodness nor badness, neither opportunity for moral merit nor the chance of proving one's conviction by sacrificing one's desires to what one thinks right. Only where we ourselves are responsible for our own interests and are free to sacrifice them has our decision moral value. We are neither entitled to be unselfish at someone else's expense nor is there any merit in being unselfish if we have no choice. The members of a society who in all respects are made to do the good things have no title to praise."

- F.A. Hayek

Agency cuts both ways. When one is alleviated of all responsibility for their decisions, they deserve no commendation for being coerced into doing what may seem right. The societal right to hold individuals responsible for what they do wrong is a pre-condition for one to be rewarded in doing right.

SOCIAL-
ISM

"The champions of socialism call themselves progressives, but they recommend a system which is characterized by rigid observance of routine and by a resistance to every kind of improvement. They call themselves liberals, but they are intent upon abolishing liberty. They call themselves democrats, but they yearn for dictatorship. They call themselves revolutionaries, but they want to make the government omnipotent. They promise the blessings of the Garden of Eden, but they plan to transform the world into a gigantic post office. Every man but one a subordinate clerk in a bureau."

- *Ludwig Von Mises*

The fatal mistake many defenders of free markets and classical liberalism make is they grant the premises so many socialists make, even as they offer counter-conclusions. At its core, socialism is not a well-intentioned belief system that simply lacks efficiency or follow-through. The internal contradictions in its belief system are numerous, and the disastrous conclusions that come out of it are a result of its foundations, not despite its foundations.

"The principle that the end justifies the means is in individualist ethics regarded as the denial of all morals. In collectivist ethics it becomes necessarily the supreme rule."

- F.A. Hayek

This is the unsolvable moral dilemma for socialism. It applies to the society as a whole an ethic that we intuitively know to be unethical in our individual lives.

"One of the most important reasons for studying history is that virtually every stupid idea that is in vogue today has been tried before and proved disastrous before, time and again."

- Thomas Sowell

21st century advocates of socialism would do well to study the consequences of 20th century socialism.

"Under capitalism, man oppresses man. But under socialism, it's the other way around."

- Russ Roberts

This is one of my favorite quotes in all of economics, not just for its wit and snark. It makes (through wit and snark) the most profound point in the entire Smith/Marx divide: The collectivists have not helped us avoid the dark side of the human condition that they fear in a market economy; they have simply replaced the bad actor with a disinterested third party at best—and a totalitarian monster at worst.

"For reasons I do not entirely understand, the clerisy after 1848 turned toward nationalism and socialism, and against liberalism, and came also to delight in an ever-expanding list of pessimisms about the way we live now in our approximately liberal societies. ... Antiliberal utopias believed to offset the pessimisms have been popular among the clerisy. Its pessimistic and utopian books have sold millions. But the twentieth-century experiments of nationalism and socialism, of syndicalism in factories and central planning for investment, of proliferating regulation for imagined but not factually documented imperfections in the market, did not work. And most of the pessimisms about how we live now have proven to be mistaken. It is a puzzle. Perhaps you yourself still believe in nationalism or socialism or proliferating regulation. And perhaps you are in the grip of pessimism about growth or consumerism or the environment or inequality. Please, for the good of the wretched of the earth, reconsider."

- Deirdre N. McCloskey

I can scarcely add to the wisdom and beauty of this plea! Pessimism has been a failed ideology, has given birth to utopian failures, and has left carnage in its wake. Liberal societies are the antidote to utopianism, and the free and virtuous society cannot happen without a rejection of the failures of pessimism, and subsequently, a rejection of the utopian socialisms that have come next.

"One of the great mistakes is to judge policies and programs by their intentions rather than their results."

- Milton Friedman

I am not going to grant that all socialist endeavors have had great intentions. The vast majority have not. But where public sympathy for the battle cry of the collectivist lies—that they merely want equality and more shared blessings amongst the under-privileged—we must do the hard work of analyzing how even the results of such intentions have played out. It is here that collectivism receives an even worse grade.

"Unquestionably, the promise of more freedom was responsible for luring more and more liberals along the socialist road, for blinding them to the conflict which exists between the basic principles of socialism and liberalism, and for often enabling socialists to usurp the very name of the old party of freedom. Socialism was embraced by the greater part of the intelligentsia as the apparent heir of the liberal tradition; therefore, it is not surprising that to them the idea of socialism's leading to the opposite of liberty should appear inconceivable."

- F.A. Hayek

Incorrigibility is a dangerous thing when you are talking about ideologies intended to govern the affairs of the world.

"Socialism in general has a record of failure so blatant that only an intellectual could ignore or evade it."

- *Thomas Sowell*

For all of the moral and economic arguments I will make against socialism, one would think the mere testimony of history would render the conversation obsolete. Quite the contrary! Despite a century of abysmal and often unspeakable results, the intelligentsia has kept the failed theory alive. One can be forgiven for wondering why that may be—is it a genuine yet stubborn belief in the ability of a chosen few to command the affairs of the economy for everyone else? Or, is it the desire to be in the chosen few, who command the affairs of the economy for everyone else?

"People commit fraud both in and out of businesses, and the evidence shows they are just as dishonest outside of a business context as within it."

- *Tyler Cowen*

The premise that socialism or collectivism or any heavy command-control economy will purge us of the ills of human nature embedded in the profit motive ignores one crucial and painful reality: Human nature is not side-stepped when the pursuit is power, any more than it is when the pursuit is profit.

"The standard wealth-redistribution policies that are often regarded as indispensable to poverty alleviation have failed to achieve their goals. Hence it behooves all Catholics to ask ourselves why such approaches have failed if we're going to have a serious conversation about wealth and poverty in the modern world."

- Dr. Samuel Gregg

This is not merely an indictment of socialism, and perhaps not even primarily one. It is an indictment of the Great Society, of the Welfare State, and of the entire idea that compulsory wealth redistribution is the cure for poverty. The reason for the failure of redistributionist strategies is that they misdiagnose the problem (believing it to be the allocation of wealth instead of participation in wealth-building activities), and because wealth redistribution does not capture the fundamental problem we seek to cure—namely, respect for the dignity of the individual as made in the image of God. Not only is curing the tragedy of poverty by creating dependency futile, it is replacing one tragedy with another.

"The first lesson of economics is scarcity: There is never enough of anything to satisfy all those who want it. The first lesson of politics is to disregard the first lesson of economics."

- Thomas Sowell

The tragedy of the political world is that more can be advanced politically by ignoring economic truth than by embracing it. That scarcity is at the heart of economics, and that all allocation of scarce resources involves trade-offs, is one of the rare indisputable laws of economics. And yet in political frameworks, it is explicitly denied to the point of absurdity.

CAPITAL ALLO-CATION

"It's very hard to argue in logical terms that spending money unwisely is the way to get wealthy."

- Russ Roberts

This is perhaps as simple a refutation of Keynesianism as you will find (though many simple refutations on many different fronts will be found in this book). But because an honest encapsulation of one of the basic tenets of Keynesianism is that unwise, unnecessary spending can be a great promotion of the public good via manipulation of aggregate demand, it is necessary for us to reduce the tenet to its real logical conclusion—that somehow spending money foolishly will create a non-foolish result. It deserves the scorn inferred in Roberts' quote.

"The fact that the market is not doing what we wish it would do is no reason to automatically assume that the government would do better."

- Thomas Sowell

When we think about the way that resources are allocated in a market economy, we do not need to assume "perfection." I can easily imagine any number of scenarios where I from my imperfect vantage point may believe capital could have been allocated more efficiently (though it should surprise no one that my own assessment is likely colored by self-interest, bias, or even just plain ignorance in a given transaction). The error of the collectivist is to take this individual hunch and parlay it into capital allocation decisions that belong to a disinterested third party—and one marinated in inefficient bureaucracy at that—the government.

"Nobody spends somebody else's money as carefully as he spends his own. Nobody uses somebody else's resources as carefully as he uses his own. So if you want efficiency and effectiveness, if you want knowledge to be properly utilized, you have to do it through the means of private property."

- Milton Friedman

Here we see the undeniable utilitarian reality around private property—a concept rooted in the very notion of subsidiarity itself, carried out to its glorious logical conclusions—optimal resource allocation comes from people caring for their own property. This has greater ramifications than just the way in which someone will be more careful with their own goods than a disinterested third party would. It speaks to the entire ecosystem of resource allocation—that each person holding, stewarding, nurturing, cultivating, considering, and perhaps liquidating their own assets, resources, and property, will affect a wiser and more efficient process and result than any possible alternative.

"Supply creates its own demand."

- Jean-Baptiste Say

The birth of supply-side economics is captured in this world-changing line, but it was uttered in the early 1800s. And Say's law is not just an underlying premise to supply-side thinking, but it represents the most meaningful elaboration to classical economics since Adam Smith.

"Say's Law, which was kind of the bedrock proposition of classical economics...is that production creates its own demand; in other words, that the economy is a cyclical kind of process. If you produce something you pay money.... The widget makers pay their employees to make the widgets, and the employees use their compensation to buy widgets. If you extend this over an economy and over a great number and great variety of goods, you have a picture of an economy."

- Robert L. Bartley

Before there was a supply-side movement, there was Jean Baptiste Say and Say's Law. A production (or supply) focused view of the economy emphasizes production, contrary to the Keynesian view that emphasizes demand. Say's Law was economic, in so much as it focused on the economic cyclicality of paying people to produce, which drove their own consumption. He was not wrong.

My view of a production-focused view of the economy adds the existential element—that man was created to produce, and consumption comes only out of our production. We can only consume after we have first produced, and we can only consume what someone else first produced. This not only creates a virtuous cycle economically, as Bartley refers to above, but you honor mankind's dignity and drive usefulness, productivity, and purpose.

"What the banking system needs is creditors who monitor risk and cut their exposure when that risk is too high. Unlike regulators, creditors and counterparties know the details of a deal and have their own money on the line."

- Tyler Cowen

You can call this principle the "skin in the game" principle, and it is not just at the root of mitigating individual risk, but also eliminating systemic risk.

"The essential difference between rich societies and poor societies...arises mainly from the fact that rich nations possess a more extensive network of capital goods wisely invested from an entrepreneurial standpoint. These goods consists of machines, tools, computers, buildings, semi-manufactured goods, software, etc., and they exist due to prior savings of the nation's citizens. In other words, comparatively rich societies possess more wealth because they have more time accumulated in the form of capital goods, which places them closer in time to the achievement of much more valuable goals."

- Jesús Huerta de Soto

The allocation of resources that stems from capital formation is a miracle of markets that feeds on itself unless policymakers interfere to destroy the miracle. A productive and entrepreneurial nation accumulates capital goods over time. A productive and entrepreneurial nation accumulates savings. Savings, capital goods, and investment are the fruits of wealth, and its sustenance.

"[Regarding the 'paradox of thrift'], there is no paradox here; Keynes is wrong. It is prudent for families facing job loss to put something away. It is also prudent for a society that has overspent and overborrowed to start saving. This is true with or without an economic slump."

- *Hunter Lewis*

Ultimately, allowing Keynesianism to get away with the presentation of "savings" as problematic leads to a continuation of a feedback loop that simply has to be broken. From the outset, the principle of savings—and the character trait of thrift—should be celebrated. That in an economic downturn, over-indebted societies suffer worse as such over-indebtedness leads to pulling back on spending even more, may be obvious (and even unfortunate). But blaming the problem on the pulling back of spending rather than on the over-indebtedness that caused the downturn, and then exacerbated the pull back, is like blaming the car for swerving out of the way when there are hazards on the road. Let's remove the hazards, and let's fix the road. But the car has to do what the car has to do.

DIVI-
SION
OF
LABOR

"It is the maxim of every prudent master of a family, never to attempt to make at home what it will cost him more to make than to buy.... What is prudence in the conduct of every private family, can scarce be folly in that of a great kingdom."

- Adam Smith

Perhaps the most famous quote on the concept of division of labor in human history... But the message here is profound and crucial to our understanding. Out of the simplicity of this basic concept comes the complexity of specialization. And out of this complexity has come more prosperity and wealth creation than anything the world has ever seen.

"The division of labor...made possible enormous improvements in the efficiency and quality of production. Dividing and subdividing manufacturing processes into specialized tasks saves a great deal of time and effort, and more important, it creates greater specialization and expertise. Rather than each man knowing a little about a lot, each becomes an expert in something in particular and sells his expertise to others in return for money or someone else's expertise. That way, all work is done by specialists, and so is done better. And because each person can trade on the value of his expertise, he has added reason to improve his prowess and his products."

- Yuval Levin

A truly articulate way of laying out the "1+1=3" reality of the division of labor. Incentives matter, and when one has a specialization that fits into the supply chain of a needed product or service, they are incentivized to continually improve upon that specialization. It is a virtuous cycle at work. We not only cannot build or do certain things if everyone's contributions were the same, but we would create no differentiation in the marketplace and would strip creativity and excellence from the process.

"Specialization is both the cause and the effect of prosperity, and it creates the modern economic life that allows us to move beyond subsistence. Small groups of people—no matter how talented, no matter how skilled or strong or smart—cannot be wealthy by modern standards over any sustained period of time."

- Russ Roberts

The interesting point here is not merely the progress that a division of labor and specialization undoubtedly creates, but the unsustainability of any progress that could ever come without it. A large and complex world has become monumentally productive because a lot of people exert themselves individually, to their own skill, calling, and ability.

"We owe the origin and development of human society and, consequently, of culture and civilization, to the fact that work performed under the division of labor is more productive than when performed in isolation."

- Ludwig Von Mises

At each point in human history that we see major and definable and significant steps forward in the progress of civilization—in the quality of life of people—there was some manifestation of division of labor at work.

"All trades, arts, and handiworks have gained by division of labour, namely, when, instead of one man doing everything, each confines himself to a certain kind of work distinct from others in the treatment it requires, so as to be able to perform it with greater facility and in the greatest perfection. Where the different kinds of work are not distinguished and divided, where everyone is a jack-of-all-trades, there manufactures remain still in the greatest barbarism."

- Immanuel Kant

Sameness is the enemy of creativity, and it is the enemy of productivity. Diversity here actually has a real meaning, not virtue-signaling noise. But the concept of diversity here refers to distinction, specialization, differentiation, unique creativity, focused talent and skill—all creating an improving output against the spirit of mediocrity that no division of labor fosters.

"Every step by which an individual substitutes concerted action for isolated action results in an immediate and recognizable improvement in his conditions. The advantages derived from peaceful cooperation and division of labor are universal."

- *Ludwig Von Mises*

The great Austrian economist was masterful in pointing out the propensity for peace to break out wherever mankind worked together towards a common aim, with each person's contribution distinct yet vital to the end goal. Those cooperative benefits combined with the improvements a division of labor represents for the process, the workers, and the consumer all serve as the foundation of this magnificent addition to free enterprise.

"Under a system of perfectly free commerce, each country naturally devotes its capital and labor to such employments as are most beneficial to each. This pursuit of individual advantage is admirably connected with the universal good of the whole. By stimulating industry, by rewarding ingenuity, and by using most efficaciously the peculiar powers bestowed by nature, it distributes labor most effectively and most economically, while by increasing the general mass of productions, it diffuses general benefit and binds together by one common tie of interest and intercourse, the universal society of nations throughout the civilized world."

- David Ricardo

This concept is, of course, at the heart of free trade as well. The diversity of talent that exists in a free society is expanded upon when we consider global taste, experience, skill, and ingenuity. Harnessing the division of labor across countries has allowed the free enterprise system leverage in spreading its rewards.

There are, of course, critics of the idea that a division of labor across the global landscape is good for domestic interests. Questions of shared cultural values are raised that are not easily answered by market mechanisms. It is here that a simple but mysteriously ignored appeal to the free *and virtuous* society is paramount. That free exchange or harnessing the division of labor would *force* a business to transact with evil actors is absurd. A failure of conscience is not a failure of a market economy; it is a failure of a bad actor created with agency.

VIRTUE & DISCIP-LINE

"As it turns out, our capitalist age is generally not an age of discipline. Far from it: Our society in most respects is a study in unbounded appetite. Our chief public-health problem is obesity. Our foremost social pathologies result from an absence of sexual restraint and personal responsibility. Our popular culture much of the time is a diabolical mix of Babylonian decadence and Philistine vulgarity. And our public life is a gluttonous feast upon the flesh of the future—we use more than we need, spend more than we have, and borrow more than we can pay. For all of our immense wealth, we somehow manage to live far beyond our means. In fact, it is almost fair to say that we lack for nothing except discipline."

- Yuval Levin

No proponent of free enterprise can ever presume the sufficiency of the market in restraining carnal appetites. There are character traits that enable humans to flourish—integrity, discipline, patience, humility, delayed gratification. And the absence of these character traits goes a long way towards undermining human flourishing. The case for free enterprise is not that it assures us of character. Rather, good character facilitates our efforts in free enterprise; good character is rewarded by free enterprise. And just as a lack of freedom undermines the quest for character, so a lack of character undermines our efforts in a free economy. The free *and* virtuous society—both free and virtuous—must be our aim.

"Being trustworthy and honest maintains and helps to extend the culture of decency beyond your own reach. You are part of a system of norms and informal rules that is much bigger than yourself. When you behave with virtue you are helping to sustain that system.... Every time you reward someone's trust or go the extra mile, you are encouraging others to do the same."

- Russ Roberts

There is an infectiousness to virtuous behavior. Not only does it serve as an example to others, but it helps reinforce the norms that make civilization possible.

"It is true that the virtues which are less esteemed and practiced now—independence, self-reliance, and the willingness to bear risks, the readiness to back one's own conviction against a majority, and the willingness to voluntary cooperation with one's neighbors—are essentially those on which an individualist society rests. Collectivism has nothing to put in their place, and in so far as it already has destroyed then it has left a void filled by nothing but the demand for obedience and the compulsion of the individual to what is collectively decided to be good."

- *F.A. Hayek*

The vision for a free and virtuous society rejects the collectivist vision and yet relies on the hope, prayer, and necessity of the virtues embedded in individuals that can make this vision reality—self-government, courage, and individual responsibility.

"Capitalism offers nothing but frustrations and rebuffs to those who wish—because of claimed superiority of intelligence, birth, credentials, or ideals—to get without giving, to take without risking, to profit without sacrifice, to be exalted without humbling themselves to understand others and meet their needs."

- George Gilder

The character trait of listening enhances the skill of the entrepreneur. Empathy is rewarded in free enterprise; aloofness is punished. These disciplines start with humility and feed the positive feedback loop that is the free and virtuous society.

"Moreover, an economics of growth and an ethic of restraint make for an awkward match, and the disciplining signals of the market alone are not enough to bridge the gap. [We would be] mistaken to assume that capitalism could produce sufficient moral authority to provide that balance on its own. Such authority would have to come from more traditional moral and cultural institutions beyond the market. And our case for capitalism must therefore also be a case for those institutions—for the family, and for religion and tradition. Democratic capitalism at its best combines the strengths of these institutions with the power of the market."

- Yuval Levin

The tragedy in the way so many modern advocates of free enterprise make their case is their willful dismissal of the institutions needed to effect restraint and virtue in our market activities. Strong families, strong churches, and strong civic life is not an elective for a market economy. Deterioration in such mediating institutions will mean deterioration in the capacity of the market to effect growth, prosperity, and human flourishing. No market advocate is ever a collectivist, as Rousseauian collectivism is the great enemy of human dignity. *But no market advocate is ever a radical individualist, either*. Rather, our individualism must place a high value on the mediating institutions of family, church, and civil society.

"[Our case is] for the moderate virtues, encouraged by market pressures but finally drawn from deeper wells— from the wisdom of tradition, the love of the family, and the divine and mysterious tug of a love beyond love, all of which must in turn be supported, encouraged, and strengthened. This is perhaps the most daunting challenge confronting the friends of capitalism today.

Our purpose is to protect and strengthen our way of life, to stand up for a social and economic system that has lifted billions out of poverty and vastly improved our world in countless ways, and to avert a careless slide toward social-democratic melancholy and decline.... [Ours] is an argument for individual freedom amid moral order, and for prosperity sustained by sympathy and discipline. It is an odd modern hybrid: a conservative case for the liberal society. As such, it is also an integral piece of the case for America."

- Yuval Levin

The deeper wells of which he speaks are not luxuries; they are necessities for a liberal society. The secular enlightenment failed to understand that the beginning of knowledge is the fear of the Lord. Likewise, secular market economists fail to appreciate that the great objectives of a market economy are not sustainable without being married to what is the beginning of freedom—the transcendent truths that give us the basis for love.

"One important characteristic of civilization is trust. When you can trust the people you deal with—when you don't have to fear that your trust will be exploited for someone else's gain—life is lovelier and economic life is much easier. How does trust get created? By the myriad small interactions we have with each other when we honor our word and pass up the chance for opportunism."

- Russ Roberts

This is the positive feedback loop of a free and virtuous society at its finest. Market interactions are more frequent and more substantive—greater exchange (and wealth creation) out of greater confidence—stemming from the trust that is earned through credible market transactions. Do well by each other, and you will do more doing well by each other.

"Work supplies the physical, psychological, artistic, and religious needs of communities extending to the ends of the earth. Furthermore, through work, we create abundance out of which we help meet the needs of others."

- Victor Claar

There is no mechanism I have seen that more cultivates personal virtue or brings greater service to mankind than work. In work we can find purpose. We can meet the most selfish needs of our inner selves—that is, the deployment of our time, the achievement of our goals, the demonstration of our capabilities—and yet, all the while achieve the most unselfish of aims—the service of others. *Work* (in human action) *is the verb of economics.*

CONCLUSION

The "categories" around which this book is organized are significant and intentional.

The book began in the subject of **Human Flourishing** because it is the aim of economics—the *telos*—for those who understand economics the way it should be understood.

I moved into **Human Action** from there because I believe economists who do not see the reality of humans acting as the base of economic activity understand very little in the field. They can always get something right accidentally, but the human person as the core of "household management of resources" is foundational to the way we understand everything.

When we talk about **Covetousness & Class Envy**, we are acknowledging the spiritual nature of economics. Class envy passes for economic theory far too often, and diagnosing the spiritual malady that creates it will at least allow people to be intellectually honest about where certain ideas are derived.

The **Knowledge Problem** is not as esoteric or philosophical as it sounds. It is an observation that carries profound application in any number of areas. What remains unforgivable in modern economics is not a disagreement with the knowledge problem; it is that so many most certainly agree with it, and yet discard it all the time in matters of application.

When one understands all that the price mechanism represents, they will not see **Price Discovery** as an obscure concept to arbitrarily defend. Rather, it would lead to a vigorous and unrelenting campaign to defend price discovery, versus the complacent willingness to distort prices that we constantly see today.

If we teach that operating in **Self-Interest** is intrinsically evil, we will ruin civilization. And if we teach that our own self-interest is all there is to economics, we will ruin civilization.

Government Spending & Debt is presented as the primary issue of our day, and for good reason. But to understand the economic dynamics of debt, one must understand the economic ramifications of the size of government. And if the size of government is inversely related to the self-government of the people, one can understand why **Virtue & Discipline** matter so much to our study.

A defense of **Free Trade**, properly understood, is really a condemnation of **Crony Capitalism**. The belief in free trade leads to a defensible defense of freedom in setting prices, including the price of labor. **Minimum Wage** laws are but one social application of economic theory, but they are ground zero in the subject of free exchange and price discovery.

Most problems in contemporary monetary policy stem from the belief that monetary policy should be used as a tool to neutralize difficulties from the business cycle. More economic fallacies have come from resisting **Creative Destruction** than almost anything else. You can see where our understanding of so many of these topics is intertwined with our understanding of the others.

Incentives are implied in human action. Like the knowledge problem, serious economists know that incentives matter, but they advocate policies that discard the importance of incentives, and they do it self-consciously. Formulating policies of **Taxation** without regard for Incentives is like setting rules for cars without regard for pedestrians.

Credit and Sound Money are complicated subjects that many cannot resist trying to reduce to mere sound bites. There are key principles that can be mastered but too many people believe things that are wrong or incomplete and they formulate elaborate beliefs from these wrong or incomplete understandings. I wanted this economic subject to be primary in the book even though I had no chance of solving every inquiry these subjects produce. A strong foundation here allows a really cogent development of monetary theory—but the opposite leads to economic practice that has done immeasurable harm to society.

One derives a view of **Political Power** out of their view of **Social Organization**. The political is but one subset of the broader subject, and all carry serious implications for economic living. The great economic masters have always understood that a philosophy of how society is organized is where economic systems come from—not the opposite. **Socialism** is a dangerous political system because it stems from a dangerous belief about societal cooperation.

My first book was called *Crisis of Responsibility* because the subject of **Individual Responsibility** means everything to me. It is the fuel of sound economics, and its demise is supported by debunked economics. A deficient view of responsibility and dangerous economic ideas feed off of each other and wreak havoc along the way.

If all there was to economics was **Capital Allocation**, I would still love economics. The efficient and optimal allocation of capital excites me because it creates positive feedback loops in human flourishing. It generates rewards, and those rewards allocate capital more efficiently.

Likewise, the **Division of Labor** is a mere tool in economics, not its essence. Like efficient allocation of capital, the optimal specialization of labor creates one virtuous cycle after another.

And once we are done studying all these foundational components of economics, and application studies in economics, we
find ourselves back again at the purpose of it all, the cause of
human flourishing.

My hope and prayer is that your study of economics leads you
to the ideas and applications that most faithfully pursue that aim.
One who has truly learned all the subjects I focused on in this
book will not necessarily have a comprehensive and systematic
understanding of economics. There are more mathematical, scientific, philosophical, and social studies to be had.

But I do believe one who masters these silos will be able to
master the concept of human flourishing. That is the aim of this
book—to provide the *first principles* necessary to advocate for
that cause.

If you can master that, but still want to go deeper into systematic
economics, I will write another book.

But if you master the first principles contained herein on the
subjects I organized this book around, you will be prepared to
champion the cause of human flourishing.

And that will leave you miles ahead of modern economists.

ACKNOWLEDGMENTS

This book would not have been possible without the loving, sacrificial, and gracious support of my wife, Joleen. If economics is human action, Joleen is the most significant economic contributor in my life, for her actions have enabled my work to succeed and my dreams to come true. She is the great love of my life, and I remain in daily gratitude for her sacrifice and support.

Besides my friends for whom this book is dedicated, Eric Balmer and Aaron Bradford, I do owe incredible gratitude to my friends that have joined me in a lifetime intellectual journey: Luis Garcia, Andrew Sandlin, Brian Mattson, Jeffery Ventrella, David O'Neil, Keith Carlson, Scott Baugh, Michael McClellan, Paul Murphy, Will Swaim, Tim Busch, *and so many more.* I value you all first and foremost as friends, but in this paragraph, as co-sojourners in this journey.

I miss you, Brian Harrington, every day.

I have to thank those who have most fed my journey with motivation, information, inspiration, and example. Many of the people I quote in this book are long gone, but they were tremendous intellectual influences, something I will never take for granted. Many of them changed the course of history. But I owe special gratitude to Father Robert Sirico, who has championed the cause in a profound way in my life, and whose Acton Institute stands engaged in this great moral fight.

I am grateful that *National Review,* still standing athwart history, has embraced the truth that *capital matters,* and I look forward to years more of fighting the good fight together.

May the entire board, faculty, administration, and student body (past, present, and future) of Pacifica Christian High School learn and apply the beauty of grace and truth in a market economy.

I thank the entire family of The Bahnsen Group, co-laborers in our own journey of enterprise. Few know better than we do this basic reality of markets: *We do well, by doing good.*

I pray that my three children, Mitchell, Sadie, and Graham, would hold fast to the miracle of free enterprise, which has dramatically altered the direction of their lives, whether they now can see and appreciate that or not. And may their lives be filled with opportunities for production, not merely consumption.

And finally, I thank the God who created me in his image, and who expects of me stewardship, cultivation, and productivity. May I work harder today than I did yesterday, not to fulfill an empty conceit, but because in such a work I flourish, and lacking such work, civilization crumbles.

RECOMMENDED READING

Human Action – Ludwig von Mises

Economics in One Lesson – Henry Hazlitt

The Road to Serfdom – Friedrich Hayek

Free to Choose – Milton Friedman

Wealth and Poverty – George Gilder

The Wealth of Nations – Adam Smith

Defending the Free Market – Father Robert Sirico

Basic Economics – Thomas Sowell

Race & Economics – Walter E. Williams

The Law – Frédéric Bastiat

Intellectuals and Society – Thomas Sowell

Capitalism, Socialism, and Democracy – Joseph Schumpeter

The Fatal Conceit – Friedrich Hayek

Bourgeois Equality: How Ideas, Not Capital or Institutions, Enriched the World – Deirdre McCloskey

Foundations of a Free & Virtuous Society – Dylan Pahman

Capitalism and Freedom – Milton Friedman

Principles of Economics – Carl Menger

Econoclasts – Brian Domitrivic

The Commercial Society – Samuel Gregg

ABOUT THE AUTHOR

David L. Bahnsen is the founder, Managing Partner, and Chief Investment Officer of The Bahnsen Group, managing over $3 billion of client capital. He is a regular guest on Fox Business, CNBC, and Bloomberg, and he is annually recognized as one of the top wealth advisors in the country by *Barron's*, *Forbes*, and *Financial Times*.

He is the author of the weekly investment commentary, *DividendCafe.com*, as well as the daily economic bulletin, *theDCtoday.com*, He hosts the weekly *Capital Record* podcast at National Review.

David and his wife of twenty years, Joleen, live bi-coastally in Newport Beach, CA and New York City. They have three children, Mitchell, Sadie, and Graham. David is a founding trustee of Pacifica Christian High School in Orange County and a trustee at the National Review Institute. In his spare time, he enjoys reading, writing, and USC football.

www.thebahnsengroup.com
www.bahnsen.com